# Insight *through* Intuition

12.99

JULIE SOSKIN

# *Insight* through

## THE PATHWAY TO

# Intuition

## SPIRITUAL SELF-DEVELOPMENT

CARROLL & BROWN PUBLISHERS LIMITED

First published in 2005 in the United Kingdom by

Carroll & Brown Publishers Limited
20 Lonsdale Road
London NW6 6RD

Managing Art  Editor Emily Cook
Illustrator  Rupert Soskin

A CIP catalogue record for this book is available from the British Library.

ISBN 1-904760-22-8

10987654321

Reproduced by RALI, Spain
Printed and bound in Italy by Eurolitho

# Contents

# Chapter 1

## Background to spiritual self-development

*In this chapter there are some current theories about*

*spiritual self-awareness and the various definitions of terms*

*and processes most commonly linked with it. Important*

*concepts include attunement to subtle healing energies and*

*communication with spirit both within and outside the self.*

# The journey to self

Spiritual development can be seen as an adventure, one where the individual is the hero or heroine of his or her own life. Like most adventures, it takes courage to embark on it, as it requires honesty and an exploration of self and, like any gripping story, it will have its good and bad times. Often the process may feel as though you are opening a 'Pandora's box' with no idea of what you may find inside. Yet many students of spiritual development express that they feel an inner pull, a vital need to explore, wherever it may lead. In a sense, spiritual discovery is about the very meaning of life, not just the roles we play, i.e. being a mother or father; the work we do or the status we hold in society, but who we truly are. It encompasses deep questions about the meaning of life and living and as such could be described as the greatest and most important journey of all. The spiritual pathway is not for the faint hearted but it is not just hard work; it is also fun, exciting, and joyful. The value of this voyage of discovery is also the adventure itself. What will happen? What will I find? Who will I become? It can be a challenging and a deeply rewarding task.

Because by its nature it revolves around the self, any true development has to be experiential. In other words, we have to live it; not in our head, mind, or even our heart, but in the reality of every hour of every day. Like any relationship, getting to know a person is enthralling and exciting and what better person to get to know than oneself? The journey is a process of unfoldment of self, uncovering the extraneous aspects of the individual so he or she is taken deeper into his or her real core, essence, or spirit.

In the first part of this book, I look at the meaning of the associated concepts and background to spirituality. I explore constructs and theories that are currently being propounded in spiritual literature and science. Contemporary methods of spiritual development recognize the needs of the individual and how he or she understands his or her own truth, so the book is interspersed with authentic experiences from students of their own spiritual processing.

This book does not set out to convert anyone to any set of beliefs; contemporary spirituality is cross-culture and religion. It does, however, ask us to look at our beliefs, mind-sets, and any patterns that may no longer serve. It is important to question everything. What might work for another person may not work for you, and that does not mean something is right or wrong. In one sense there is no right and wrong, only the truth of who you are. We are all different, with different perspectives on life. These have been brought about by our upbringing, education, the society in which we live, and our individual experiences, which are unlikely to tally completely with any other living soul. Therefore, the spiritual journey is completely individual. Written on the ancient Greek Oracle at Delphi were the words "Know thyself." To do this requires integrity of one's truth and yet many people do not even know what their real truth is, but go blindly through life. This book can be taken on many different levels but its aim is to promote thought and explore spiritual perspectives; where that leads is up to you.

# Spirituality

Spiritual generally relates to the non-physical, and can be thought of as a state that lies beyond physical reality. Spirituality also can refer to an awareness of one's inner self, and a sense of connection to a higher energy or power. It might be perceived to be associated with religion, but need not be connected to any. It has been described as the way we orient ourselves toward the divine, and is also described as a personal connection to the universe. Conversely, religion could be described as a doctrinal framework that guides sacred beliefs and practices, helping to structure the way people worship. Being spiritual does not necessitate having any set faith or model; indeed, the ambiguous nature of the concept is often taken to mean something outside religious context, referring to ultimate meanings and values in life.

There are various differing opinions on the meaning of spirituality but one of the commonalities in recent literature is that there is a difference between religion and spirituality. Religion means to tie together and is therefore seen as the organization of spirituality and facilitates making meaning of our world. Religion usually has a set structure that teaches people about God ("universal light force energy" or "all that is") and the way in which to live their lives. Therefore, it need not be a personal lived experience but a set of values to underpin society, life, and living.

In the context used within this work, spiritual is not confined to any particular religion or dogma, but rather it is used according to its

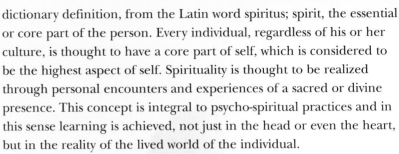

dictionary definition, from the Latin word spiritus; spirit, the essential or core part of the person. Every individual, regardless of his or her culture, is thought to have a core part of self, which is considered to be the highest aspect of self. Spirituality is thought to be realized through personal encounters and experiences of a sacred or divine presence. This concept is integral to psycho-spiritual practices and in this sense learning is achieved, not just in the head or even the heart, but in the reality of the lived world of the individual.

Spirit might be thought of as the vital life force, which motivates people and influences life, health, behaviour and relationships. However, spirituality is not just thought to be an inner quality. It also can be a way of understanding your relationship and connection to something outside of your self that provides meaning.

Although individuals may identify the spiritual sense as something that could be either an external or internal experience, these do not have to be mutually exclusive. In spiritual development, the individual is usually thought to link to a higher power, which is generally accessed through the deepest core of self; however, there also can be a connection with a higher power outside the self.

Acclaimed biologist Alister Hardy, drawing from the fields of psychology, animal behaviour, psychic research and anthropology, propounds the hypothesis that: "Spirituality is natural to the human species and has evolved because it has biological survival value." Evolving might suggest some form of purpose in the process, but Hardy seems to imply that there is a direct intuitive awareness that is ever-present or innate. This is a contentious issue, which is similar to the thorny question of whether "nature or nurture" makes the difference. Are the building blocks of spirituality within us at birth or do they develop? If the definition of spirituality is that we all have a "core" or essential part of self, it follows that spirituality is present in everyone and, like all our faculties, it therefore has the potential to be developed. In recent years, the notion of spirituality has begun to emerge outside any set structures and refers to profound inner experiences that could be characterized by such traits as awareness, energy, depth, understanding of self, a holistic outlook, intuition, courage, acceptance, and love. It also could be described as that which implements the growth of positive and creative values in the human existence.

In the past ten years we have seen an explosion of interest in diverse disciplines including education, religion, psychology, health, healing and the arts. It seems there is personal desire to get in touch with something more, something beyond the personal self, and this has spilled over into the media. It is now common to see these subjects covered in lifestyle articles and magazines. Some of these are un-authenticated and somewhat superficial; however, in the last few years there has been increased intelligent debate and discussion about the whole area and this is encouraging the emergence of spirituality as part of the mainstream agenda. Although this book defines spirituality as the core and essence of a person, it seems likely that any common definitive meaning will continue to be elusive because of the personal nature of spirituality.

**EXPERIENCE**

"*I had many years of addiction and although I was able to hold down a very demanding job it was eating into me. I was in a dark, fearful void and I was not living a life that was real or true to myself. Through spiritual practices in therapy I came to look at the deeper areas of self. For me, spirituality is being at one, with me and the rest of the world. It's looking at life from my authentic self, from my soul. The way that I look at life is from a much richer perspective today because before I would look at life just from the personality and now I don't look at life quite the same, I look at life from the deeper level of my soul and that's what I feel to be my spirituality. I have shifted, it's just a different way that I look at life. I see people at a much more deeper level — at a soul level.*

*I remember looking yesterday at a friend as a human being with so much richness and joy. My job as a crime officer took me into areas of meeting people who were very dark, but now I can look at people differently and my vision is only out of goodness and not looking for what they may or may not do or who they are or what they have done. I see them and I go right to the core of them. I also see much deeper into many things; pictures, nature and trees. You can actually see them in a different way, you can hear the music of a tree, you can hear the music in water dripping, you can hear sounds that you never thought you could hear, just in the silence. You can hear the world can't you? It's good isn't it?*"

# Contemporary spirituality

Spiritual concepts relate to qualities of life that go beyond the ordinary physical and material states – the feeling that there is something more to life. Religions have social structures and officials such as priests and elders to ensure the purity and propriety of practice. Contemporary spirituality, on the other hand, depends on the experiential journey of encounter and relationship with others – powers and forces beyond the scope of everyday life. To be spiritual is to be open to more than just the material in life, and to expect to encounter and nurture a relationship with it.

Many orthodox believers feel that finding your own spiritual truth outside a religious context is not desirable, for where is the comfort of the society, the followers and practices that have been built up over hundreds and thousands of years? Religions offer support to the community, often holding society together, and the people involved have grown and progressed as a result of their shared culture. Nonetheless, although religions and religious leaders may give support to their own "tribes" and advise moral ethics, unfortunately they also have used their ideals and teachings as excuses to carry out awful things in the name of religion. Due to the global media these incidents have become evident and have led to an increasing suspicion that religions have not always got things right. Many religious people who claim they may be ready to die for their cause may not be prepared to live in peace and harmony with their neighbours. Contemporary spirituality, however, demands authenticity, a need to "live" your beliefs, not be told what they should be.

Generally, contemporary spiritual self-development practices do not stipulate that the student has to follow any particular belief system. Rather they are sympathetic and tolerant towards any tradition, faith, or religion that aids the individual in his or her spiritual progress. These practices do, however, encourage the mystical notion of the transcendence of human understanding and the ability of the individual to communicate directly with a higher force. They also propound that spiritual unfoldment is possible for everyone.

If the whole area of spirituality is not necessarily within a set model or structure, we no longer have to be nuns, monks, or priests to access greater spiritual truths. We can become our own priest or priestess. In some ways, this makes the task harder. If you are cloistered from society it may be easier to concentrate on the spiritual aspects of self than if you have to bring your truth into the material world, your work place, and relations with family, friends and lovers. Without any set models, who is going to tell us what is right? We are now being asked to come of age spiritually, to make our own decisions and to take responsibility for them.

# Spiritual psychology

Roberto Assagioli developed a form of spiritual or "transpersonal" psychology, which he labelled "Psychosynthesis". He maintained that we all possess a super-consciousness described as the "psyche", which contains our deepest potential, the source of the unfolding pattern of our unique human path of development. This super-consciousness or deeper aspect of self continually invites us to levels of healing and wholeness, hence the prefix trans, which means beyond or above, in this case, the personal state of an individual. Transpersonal psychology can be applied to the entire spectrum of human experience; it honours the spiritual dimension of self and the deep human need for transcendental experiences.

The psychological and the spiritual might be interwoven and often cannot be separated; therefore individuals need to be seen as "psycho-spiritual units". Indeed, the words "psycho-spiritual" can be used as an alternative to "transpersonal". Psycho-spiritual and transpersonal work takes account of the fact that individuals may have aspects of self that mask deep spiritual connection and that they need to unfold, and possibly dissolve, unhelpful aspects of self to allow greater contact with the spirit within. Some of this work, therefore, necessitates looking at more psychological aspects of who we are or who we think we are. We can then loosen negative patterns so they melt away and allow us contact with the divine within.

The main focus of psycho-spirituality in this book is the development of spiritual self-awareness, and in common with transpersonal psychology it deals with aspects of the individual beyond the personal state. However, although there are many similarities between transpersonal and psycho-spiritual practices, not every transpersonalist openly embraces the worth of subtle energies, intuition, and the psychic, nor do they always utilize them as an integral part of their learning. Psycho-spirituality can draw on and acknowledge practices outside the psychology remit, such as ancient rituals, meditation, chanting and yoga.

If spirituality is innate within us how can we access it? We may need different means to look at this form of learning. People often speak of a feeling of being called or pushed with some sense of knowing. But how do we connect with this deeper sense of knowing and of what quality is this knowing? Because it is unseen and often unexplainable, it therefore requires something other than our normal means of learning.

The "sense of knowing" can be described as an unseen or intuitive sense. Developing and trusting the intuition can, therefore, be a positive advantage in the unfoldment of the spiritual self. Real intuitive spiritual work is not so much concerned with accumulating information as understanding one's own spirituality experientially. There has to be a real experience, the student has to be observant and then, by recognizing difficulties and how they manifest in his or her life, the individual is able to make changes. This is unfoldment. Later on, I will be demonstrating some useful transpersonal exercises to assist spiritual growth.

**EXPERIENCE**

"You spoke about what will was and it was suddenly my turning point. I started to think about what my true intentions really were and some of them were quite shocking but I remember thinking this is exactly how to get the balance between my will and my emotions, integration of the heart and the mind, which previously was all 'gobbley gook' to me because I was too emotionally based. My emotions were overwhelming and powerful and I was 'out of sync'. So what I learnt was, clarification and the act of will, that was a revelation and I now have a much better understanding of who I am."

# Spiritual self-awareness

The English dictionary has a long list of definitions related to the self, which describe emotional, mental, physical or spiritual aspects. In the last 20 years the vast growth in self-help groups and therapies has turned self into jargon. In psycho-spiritual studies, the spiritual aspect of self is regarded as the higher aspect of self. However, the term "higher self" is itself confusing because "higher self" also can be seen as the innate, core and soul aspect of self, which is also referred to as the inner self, nature or being. Conversely, the lower layers of self include the more mundane or known aspects i.e. the social, emotional, mental, psychological, ego or personality selves and, in contrast with the higher self, they do not necessarily make contact with the essence, spirit or soul of the person. The concept of the self in many Western cultures is generally that of the outer layers of personality and not the true inner layers. However, psychologists such as Jung, Assagioli, Rogers and Maslow have sought to incorporate this "higher" aspect of self within their work. Jung's definition of the higher self is "The God within and the individual in seeking self-realization and unity becomes the means through which God seeks his goal." Jung wrote extensively about the spiritual, seeing it as "infinite spaceless, formless imageless".

Orthodox faiths generally are uncomfortable with what they see as self-serving spirituality. The word "self" is often regarded negatively and thought to mean selfish. The word "self" might be deemed contrary to the Christian exhortation to "love thy neighbour", but this ignores the next part of the phrase, which is, "as thyself". The emphasis on compassion for the weak often ignores the positive aspects within us, and can produce dislike for strength. But in spiritual development a strong inner self that comes with maturity is vital. In contemporary spiritual practice, self-respect and self-love are not thought to remove the person from God or higher states of being but rather become the

**EXPERIENCE**

"*About twenty-eight years ago, after going through a lot of changes, including dark night of the soul I felt complete awareness of who I was, complete and total healing and complete love. Up until then I had been experiencing a lot of difficulty, psychic attacks and a lot of confusion, in a sense life was blowing through me and I seemed unable to do anything about it. I was blown around like a leaf in the winds. Up until then I hadn't any experiences, but I was looking for truth, exploring all kinds of interesting avenues. I had no real certainty of anything, until experience of spiritual development and although I didn't shift things over night it actually gave me a place to work from, to balance everything.*"

very means by which first-hand communication with a higher power is reached, and from that it is believed that the emancipation of the true inner spirit can occur.

The negative aspects of self are like veils obscuring the true inner nature or highest self, and need to be parted or drawn away as the individual journeys deeper and deeper towards the core of his or her spirit. In this book we will aim to assist this unfoldment process through experiential learning to actualize the reality of yourself as a spiritual being.

# Intuition

Intuitive information can be seen as eccentric in nature, as it rarely follows any set pattern. So given the uncertainty of this subject, why choose intuition as a navigator for a spiritual self-development programme? Is it a reliable source of truth? It could be argued there are many better ways to find one's spirituality; following a religious practice, or finding an authentic spiritual teacher, for instance, and these are often part of the spiritual process. However, because of the individual aspect of spirituality, your in(ner) tuition might assist the journey of self. That being the case, this faculty needs to be developed, for like any quality – mental, physical or intellectual – it must be possible for it to be trained.

Many indigenous peoples, prior to Western conquest, worked with what "felt" right. Tribes often existed with an intuitive rapport between their people. Their communication was spontaneous, open and honest. They spoke with truth and it worked because personal feelings were above board and accurately expressed. This, of course, requires transparency in aspiration, interest and desire. Our culture rarely promotes such transparency.

Authentic spiritual self-awareness is thought to require openness. We need therefore to ask what stands between our truths? The educationalist Peters tells us, "Our wishes and fears limit how we see the world ... (they) can lead to windowless tunnel vision, to a peep-hole on the world determined by our own preoccupations".

If fear limits our world, could it cloak our truth, and if so might it affect our communications with our inner being or self? If we throw light on our fears, negative patterns and assumptions, could it bring us closer to our inner selves and enable contact with our inner beings? Accessing intuition is thought to provide a readily accessible decision-making tool which might aid the process of unveiling aspects of our lower self, which cloak the core or true spiritual self. In accessing intuition we get closer to our true inner self.

Paraphrasing Abraham Maslow, Peters suggests our inner nature is cloaked and weak, it persists underground, unconsciously, even though denied and repressed. It speaks softly but it will be heard, even if in a distorted form. It has a dynamic force of its own pressing always for open uninhibited expression. This force is one main aspect of the will to health, the urge to identity. It is this that makes psychotherapy, education and self improvement possible in principle.

So how can we hear this soft inner voice that often is obscured? Can religious notions guide us through? Can logic discern its elusive nature? Intuition may not be all that is needed for this task but it might give us another valuable tool to access our deeper nature.

# Therapy as part of spiritual development

Recently, integrating spirituality and psychotherapy has become a significant area of interest. It is thought that the spiritual path and the therapeutic path do not need to contradict each other, in fact they can complement each other. In this situation the therapist has two roles. One is the role of psychotherapist, the other of spiritual teacher.

One could argue that combining the roles of psychotherapist and priest can present all sorts of problems, not least being that however good the training of the therapist, it might not provide him or her with the disposition to take on the role of priest or spiritual director. Previously, "being spiritual", has been part of both organized religion and contemporary spirituality's concept of learning to be your own teacher. It might lend itself to being used as a therapy. However, it has been suggested that therapists may take the place of communities and relationships that have been lost, and thus better suit the circumstances of the modern world.

Over the last 50 years the upsurge of interest in psychotherapy, together with a much greater awareness of other cultural religious practices, has led to the importance of the person being acknowledged. It is increasingly thought that a more healthy concentration on the self, far from removing the individual from God or spirit, becomes the very means of allowing a first-hand communication with a higher power. The self therefore takes centre stage in our observation and inquiry, and that is why some aspect of psychology may not just be an advantage; it might be a necessity.

Arguably the personality part of yourself is not the core, real or authentic self, and it might mask or confuse our deeper connections, which need careful teasing out with the help of an expert. Psychological inquiry looks at personal meaning, and spiritual practice looks beyond our ordinary human concerns towards the realization of the ultimate. It has been suggested that some form of psychology might assist spiritual practice by helping to shine the light of awareness into all the hidden aspects of our conditioning. This describes some form of loosening effect on the whole psyche, possibly in line with the classic notion of the dissolution of the "veils of illusion" or "unfoldment". In the process of unfoldment there often needs to be a letting go of negativity, which can be psychologically very messy and uncomfortable. This being the case, someone not trained in the psychological process may either be unable to assist or may even exacerbate the problem. I have found that in certain cases some form of therapy alongside spiritual development is advantageous.

# The new age

The New Age Movement gained momentum soon after the Second World War and accelerated into the 1960s. The educationalist, Sir George Trevelyan, who had an influential effect in the UK promoting New Age beliefs from the late 1940s up to his death in 1996 stated, "Try to change society without the inner change in man and confusion will be the sole result".

New age describes a broad group of contemporary movements, therapies and quasi-religious groups who are seeking personal self-realization. The title "new age" is, however, technically incorrect as most of the practices are not new, but derived from age-old practices. Nonetheless, the movement is generally seen to promote the concept of the importance of self as a way to higher knowledge. Autonomy and freedom are highly valued, and it is felt that authority lies with the experience of the self.

Although some new-age individuals join cults, others also go to church or are interested in Buddhism and other religions. This movement has undoubtedly had a social and cultural effect; and, in the media, it is still common to find references to the new age alongside the 1960s' "anything goes" attitude.

One might therefore question who does the teaching in new age practices. There seems to be an array of candidates, which include those within the Eastern tradition of guru or master, to anyone who wants to set himself or herself up in a workshop.

Criticism of strong guru-type leaders, which have seen some resurgence in new age circles, is that they can set up dependency with ingrained spiritual projection. Facilitator and writer John Heron says, "This can be seen as dubious in the way it is used to legitimate spiritual power over people, by telling them what an impossible, unregenerate mess they are in without direction from those who claim to know the road to liberation". Heron also is critical of Eastern practices and may well be correct that some strict systems are male-dominated. My experience over the last twenty years, however, is that the revival of ancient practices has been subdued to accommodate Western minds and also, far from being led, or indeed exclusively filled, by males, these systems attract a large percentage of female leaders and many new age writers even actively propound the "Rebirth of the Goddess".

The argument for new age practices is that there is value in the multi-variant spontaneous coming together of different faiths and practices, which puts power in the hands of the individual to find what suits him or her best. However, some new age practices are diverse and unstructured with little real desire to intelligently examine themselves. Therefore, I share some sympathy with the scepticism towards the more dubious new age practices and I would urge the genuine spiritual seeker to be discerning. Nonetheless, some of the more reputable therapies involved in the new age movement – including homeopathy, naturopathy and spiritual healing – have gone a long way in the last few years to bring themselves in line with professional standards.

# Spiritual education

In an increasing multi-cultural society the question of spiritual development and learning is a pertinent one. There is, however, some difficulty in giving content to the idea of spiritual education without identifying it with either religious or moral education. Nonetheless, there is a growing idea that spiritual education needs to include personal experience and to be open to discussion on what are described as the "big questions", i.e. the meaning of life, etc.

Recent literature says spirituality is considered a "hot topic"; there is increasing professional interest in spiritual matters paralleling that of the general public. Far from denying its presence, there has been an explosion in the number of focus groups of theological experts from diverse faiths exploring the subject. So what form can spiritual development take in a multi-cultural world? There is an argument that to have a better understanding of all faiths it is preferable to have in-depth knowledge of one. I have some sympathy with this notion as I have noticed that students who have had little or no religious education often have no frame of reference in which to evaluate their own experiences. This, however, could be perceived as a good thing as no prescriptive elements will have been indoctrinated. The students have to decipher the experiences for themselves. Perhaps we need to look into different methods and begin to teach spirituality from an open perspective accommodating and facilitating the emergence of the individual's own beliefs.

There is, however, growing recognition of the value of mystical or transcendent knowing, including some altered states of consciousness. This allows in another way of knowing – one that perhaps supersedes sensory perceptions and analysis as an effective means of knowledge. The trouble with this is that mystical experiences can be misdiagnosed and, that being the case, they could take one down very difficult paths of illusion. Nonetheless, whole new models are opening up as we look to re-engage with the spiritual nature of self.

If we accept that people see their worlds in unique ways, does it not follow they will also experience their own spiritual development in unique ways? The need to follow one's own truth seems to be gaining momentum through the desire for the genuine, and the expansion of the spiritual notion of unlimited knowledge and love. This being the case, educationalists may need to make a shift of paradigm from being exclusively rational and intellectual to experiential and intuitive. In the second part of the book we investigate this through one's own experiences.

# Chapter 2

## Where science and spirit meet

This chapter includes some interesting theories
that connect current scientific thought to spiritual and
psychic perceptions.

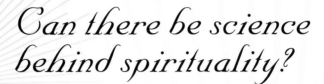

# Can there be science behind spirituality?

Can there really be a scientific explanation for a psychic "connecting with the light", or a genuine basis for the third eye? Is it possible to communicate without words and can a healer really sense another person's illness or pain?

One of the key aspects which makes psychic phenomena seem so unacceptable to science is that while people talk about different types of "energy", whether it be "healing energy", "psychic energy", "spirit energy" or "angelic forces", no psychic has ever been able to explain scientifically what sort of energy it is that he or she experiences. To scientists, energy comes in clearly defined types – heat, light, sound, electrical, chemical, nuclear – but none of them seem to apply to the descriptions of psychic experience.

The problem possibly lies in underestimating just how sensitive we really are, and how even when experiencing something tiny, it can sometimes cause us to react in a very big way. For instance, many people experience strong emotions when they hear a few bars of a piece of music, or have vivid childhood recollections when they smell something familiar, yet these strong reactions and vivid pictures are triggered by only a few sound waves or tiny molecules in the air, which cause a cascade effect in the brain allowing many connections to be lit up almost simultaneously with the relevant spark. It is like a crowd of people waiting outside a department store on the day of its big sale: it only takes one person to open the door and in seconds a thousand people have poured through, all looking for things within the store, essentially "doing" the same thing while all looking for something different.

Despite many experiments under laboratory conditions, science fnds it hard to accept any psychic phenomena as being valid. However, the more our scientific knowledge grows, the more we find the unlikeliest things occurring in nature and the universe – from particles like the *neutrino*, which stream through space, passing right through everything in their way, including our bodies, to particles which seem to be in two places at the same time. There is also the mysterious "dark matter" that accounts for 85% of the universe. Although physicists can measure it, no-one has a clue what it is. It seems the limitations lie far more in our ability to comprehend, than in any restrictions within the universe itself.

"Energy" means "a capacity for movement or change", so when we experience anything that moves us or makes us feel different, whether or not we know what it is, what we are experiencing is caused by one or more forms of energy. Whether we touch, taste, see, hear or smell, we bring all that information up to the brain in order to make sense of our environment and so everything we ever experience in our lives and the world around us is being processed internally. Our senses are the windows through which the brain sees outside our bodies, and this means that our whole world is probably shaped by the extent of our experiences and understanding. When we come into contact with something completely new, we might struggle to make any sense of it in the same way that primitive cultures with no concept of electricity, seeing our technology for the first time, might regard a torch as something magical. As it is, they only know that the torch can make light, but understanding electricity opens up a whole new world of possibilities.

We know of nothing more complex than the human brain and we have still only scratched the surface of its full potential. However, the brain, like every cell in the human body, functions by two processes, which make the whole mind-body system work: chemical and electrical. So no matter what form of energy we interact with outside of our bodies, our understanding of it comes from the chemicals and electric currents buzzing around inside our brains. A good example of how our perceptions really are interpretations is to look at sparkling lights or moving colours. What you see is the picture your brain creates from the information sent to it by your eyes. Now if you squeeze your eyes tight shut, you also may see sparkling lights and moving colours, but these are created purely from the internal workings of the brain. These two very different kinds of stimulus result in very similar interpretations. So what is happening to our minds and bodies when we have psychic experiences and what are the triggers that are so difficult for science to measure?

In the natural world, many plants and animals have capabilities that often seem like some sixth sense. Turtles who find their way through millions of square miles of open ocean to return to the beach where they were born, birds that can see the magnetic field of the earth and animals who seem to predict coming earthquakes are some examples. Even sensitivities that we understand can still seem

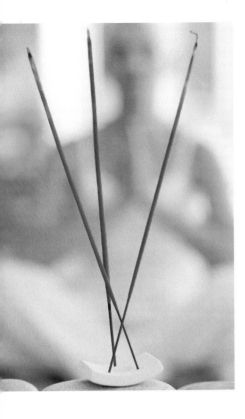

way beyond our own, like a dog's phenomenal sense of smell or a bird of prey's eyesight. Because we tend to regard ourselves as so different from other animals, we usually think our apparently limited human senses are incomparable to their greater abilities. Mother Nature, however, is rarely wasteful and if something works she will use it over and over again. Often the only difference is whether or not the stimulus is strong enough for us to be consciously aware of what is happening inside and outside our bodies, so perhaps we need to look more closely at how our bodies could be using subtle senses to do extraordinary things.

Our sense of well-being is strongly affected by our comfort and the quality of our surroundings. For instance, the reduced levels of light in winter can cause Seasonal Affective Disorder (SAD) resulting in loss of motivation and depression. We also know that changing the chemicals in the air around us – through the use of incense or perfumes – can make us calm or excited, and that different types of sound can induce every emotion – from stress and irritation with the disruptive noise of building works, to exhilaration or calm with the appropriate piece of music. If we become too hot or too cold, the body puts more effort into regulating our temperature, which in turn can cause irritability and loss of concentration.

Is it possible, therefore, that psychic ability is equally affected by the comfort of the individual, and that any outside influences which increase stress levels will in turn reduce a person's sensitivity?

# Light, colour and the chakras

Out of all our senses, we use and depend on our eyesight more than any other. We "see" because information is sent to the brain by our eyes, but vision is not the only way we experience light. What we see as visible light is only a narrow band of energy in the middle of the electromagnetic spectrum, which ranges from very high frequency waves known as gamma rays to very low frequency radio waves.

Very high frequency energy has tiny wavelengths far smaller than a billionth of a metre; as the energy slows down, the waves stretch out so that the longer radio waves are many kilometres long. Regarding the wave lengths that we recognize, we know that ultraviolet rays from the sun burn our skin and that some cookers use infrared energy. So if energy at both ends of the visible spectrum can burn us, what can be happening with the colours in between? And just because we can't "see" the faster and slower wavelengths, does that mean they don't affect us? In the natural world there are many examples of light affecting behaviour; we wouldn't be alive if plant cells didn't open and close with red and blue light to create the photosynthesis that gives us oxygen.

It is quite reasonable to describe radio waves as "slow light": after all, the only difference between the waves that burn our skin and the ones that carry our music is the speed at which they travel. When we turn on a car radio, we can drive wherever we want and continue to listen to a programme. We can start our journey next to the transmitter and drive for miles in any direction and still hear it. How? Because energy is everywhere, and we are simply driving through a sea of it while tuning in to a single point on the waves. We tune the waves through a radio set to bring them to a vibration that we can actually hear but the waves themselves surround us all the time.

Light is the same, just faster. If you stand under a clear starry sky and pick out a single star, you are looking at light that has been pouring through space for billions of miles. You can lie on the ground, go up in a plane or get in a space ship and fly towards it; the point being that you can see it anywhere because its energy is everywhere. The same applies to anything you can see. If you sit on a hillside you can look at things such as a blade of grass by your feet or a tree on the distant horizon and whilst your eyes may only be able to

*X rays Gamma rays*

*Ultra-violet radiation*

*Visible light microwaves*

*Thermal radiation radio waves*

focus on one thing at a time, the energy bouncing off all those things is bathing your body all at the same time.

It is known that some blind people can distinguish colour by touch. Much less common but just as real are people who have been blind from birth and yet can paint pictures as realistic as any sighted person. Despite having no visual experience of colour or perspective, they still perceive the world lying beyond their physical reach. It is only through viewing distant objects that we have the visual impression of things seeming to get smaller as they get closer to the horizon, so is this an example of the mind and body translating the electromagnetic information in a completely different sensory way?

Can we see and focus the wavelengths of light without the use of our eyes and is this another way the psychic feels able to connect or tune in to things?

# The chakras

The Eastern chakra system (see following chapter) traditionally comprises seven energy centres, which run in a line from the crown of the head to the base of the spine and resonate with the colours of the spectrum. In essence, the base or red centre is associated with our primal animal instincts and the centres then rise up in consciousness until the highest spiritual connection is at the violet crown. Each centre has positive and negative attributes depending on the individual's state of balance.

Colour is used extensively in marketing and manipulation because we respond to it in predictable ways. (You wouldn't want your toothpaste to come in a brown tube would you?) But apart from obvious likes and dislikes, colours actually make us feel different. Many fast food restaurants use vibrant red in their decor because, as with rich foods, we can't help being attracted to it. Surrounded by it we feel energized and alive, but like rich food, we can only take so much of it. In a relatively short space of time our senses are satisfied and we are ready to move on, ensuring a steady turnaround for the restaurant. Another example of colour being used to influence moods is painting hospital walls and prison cells in pastel shades to relax patients and calm violent prisoners. Think how different you feel when you walk in a field of bluebells as opposed to one of poppies or sunflowers.

Our spoken language intuitively associates states of mind with colour (see box right) and if we compare these with the chakra system we can see some interesting correlations (see following chapter).

At the centre of the chakra system lies the heart centre which resonates with green light. It is here that the individual is said to feel a sense of balance and harmony, where a sense of peace can be found. It is noteworthy that if we go back to the visible properties of the electromagnetic spectrum, the energy above the crown centre and below the base centre can be physically damaging to us. In exactly the same way that we will die if we become hypothermic with cold or from heat exhaustion if too hot, and we feel just right on a warm spring day, the green balance point of the chakra system and electromagnetic spectrum is also the optimum survival point for us as physical animals.

| |
|---|
| RED with anger |
| WHITE with fear |
| in the PINK |
| got the BLUES |
| GREEN with envy |
| BROWNED off |
| BLACK moods |

# Electro-sensing

Electricity is generated by the movement of the electrons orbiting around the nuclei of atoms and different types of atom have varying amounts of electrons, which makes some easier to move about than others. We use metal wires, especially copper, in all our electric appliances basically because it is the easiest substance through which to drive the movement of electrons. In our everyday lives we are only really aware of electricity as an energy when we turn our domestic appliances on and off, but it flows through our bodies every second of every day and is an essential force in every living organism. All our activity creates electricity, every movement of muscle and beat of the heart, even your brain will maintain a steady electrical current of around 10 microvolts simply by reading these pages.

It may be hard to detect but every electrical flow generates an energy field; is it, therefore, something that we can feel consciously and does this play a part in psychic experiences?

We hear performers saying that they thrive on the energy coming from an audience, that it gives them a rush of adrenaline. We sometimes describe angry people as "prickly", and often say that we can feel someone's sadness or empathize with other peoples' stress levels. Is it possible that those emotions are somehow affecting the electrical fields being generated by the body and could the

**ANIMAL "magic"**

Many animals have eyesight sensitive to wavelengths that are invisible to us. For example, birds and insects can see ultraviolet light. If you have a fish tank over your television set, every time you use the remote control, your fish can see the beam of red light flashing across the room.

differences in the electrical fields be what a psychic or healer is sensing when he or she describes a person's aura?

Sometimes we try to find answers to mysteries when the answers might be closer to hand. Every illness we ever experience is, at its basic level, a chemical imbalance. This chemical upset can be caused by the electrical functions of our cells being disturbed so the wrong balance of molecules is created. Whether it is physical or mental, the problem still manifests by the body not being able to maintain its natural state of balance. It has been shown that people, especially children, living close to power lines, can suffer disorders such as leukaemia because the strength of surrounding electrical activity disturbs the natural structure of the body's blood cells. In other situations there are increases in the occurrence of tumours. However, not all effects are detrimental and even today we still use electric shock treatment for certain psychological and brain disorders.

It could be argued that when we are comfortable we don't actually feel anything. Not too hot, not too cold, not too wet, not too dry; we are only consciously aware of outside influences when they upset our equilibrium and then we begin to feel uncomfortable.

If we keep in mind that everything we do generates electricity in our minds and bodies, is it possible that the psychic will sense things much more easily in other people when they are calm and relaxed themselves, when their own buzzing electricity is quieter?

# Chemical sensing and communication

Of all the methods of sending and receiving information in the natural world, chemical exchange is more commonplace than any other. Scent is so important that many mammals can reject their own offspring if they don't smell right. This is often observed when well-meaning people stroke young wild animals only for the animal to be rejected when the parent returns because it smells like a human. The entire cat family – from Siberian tigers to the family feline – marks its territory with scent, as do dogs, bears and many other species.

The main chemical triggers are compounds called pheromones, which, even though most animals detect them by breathing, don't actually smell very much if at all. Pheromones can affect behaviour dramatically and science has shown that we are likely to choose a mate by subconsciously analysing his or her body chemistry. Experiments demonstrate that human scents vary according to the balance of our genes and the smells we find most pleasant are those that chemically differ most from our own. It appears that we can smell the partner who can provide us with the healthiest offspring.

The ability of certain animals to detect tiny chemical changes may give us a clue to some forms of psychic sensitivity. Sharks can detect certain chemicals in solutions as low as one part per million, a male moth can detect a female from miles away on the strength of a single molecule of pheromone and many animals use similar pheromones to send out warnings of potential danger. It has long been said that animals can smell our fear, but dogs are increasingly being used medically to detect illnesses such as epilepsy, schizophrenia, diabetes and cancer through smell.

So knowing that our state of health gives off a distinct odour that is influenced by chemical changes within the body, isn't it possible that a healer can detect another person's ill health by sense of smell?

The connection between body chemistry and light could be significant in understanding some psychic faculties, especially in relation to the chakra system. Light levels are important to our natural cycles and the patterns of waking and sleeping are obvious examples of this. The pineal gland sits within the brain and has long been associated with clairvoyance and the mystical third eye. Despite it being tucked away inside the skull, it reacts to changing light levels and is responsible for regulating many of the body's cycles. Over a 24-hour cycle, as the light changes, the pineal gland secretes varying amounts of a hormone called melatonin, which peaks at night influencing the desire for sleep. The pineal gland is responsible also for triggering hibernation and breeding cycles in animals.

Is the pineal gland really the mystical "third eye" and is this another way for the psychic "to see the light" by tuning in to higher frequencies?

As with plants and all animals active during the day, our activity increases with exposure to the violet end of the spectrum arising from increased sunlight and reduces as light moves into the redder frequencies. Since we know how varying light levels affect our body chemistry, can this also explain the link between the chakras and how they relate to our state of health?

## ANIMAL "magic"

The tuatara is a nocturnal lizard-like reptile found on various islands off New Zealand and is rare in having an external "third eye" which connects directly to the pineal gland. This is only clearly seen in the young of the species and becomes covered over with scales at around four to six months old. This well-developed organ helps the young to absorb ultraviolet light, which creates vitamin D in the body.

# Body language

Throughout the whole of the animal kingdom, body language is an area rich in both conscious and subconscious signals. There are many obvious examples of aggressive and defensive displays such as animals baring their teeth, pinning back their ears or raising their eyebrows in alarm. Equally, a wagging tail or relaxed posture can immediately convey a non-threatening attitude.

With humans, a frown and a tapping foot are as clear indicators of impatience while a fisherman's arms held wide convey the size of "the one that got away". Humans constantly use subtle signals to convey specific thoughts to a friend or partner, particularly in situations where words are impossible or inappropriate; the tiniest movement of the head or a discreet wink can communicate a private thought. But how much information do we exchange through subconscious changes of expression or posture?

On another level, the autonomic nervous system that drives all the essential processes that we do not consciously control, such as breathing, heartbeat and digestion, is regulated by complex chemical changes in the body. This powerful system is responsible for many of our involuntary actions like blushing and dilation of the pupils, which often display emotions we would far rather be keeping to ourselves.

Does the psychic unconsciously derive information by reading the subtle signals of unconscious and autonomic body language?

Our unconscious body language is often a clear indicator of our state of mind and can sometimes give away more than we would like. We tend to have an unconscious but nonetheless clearly defined area of "personal space", which is usually around an arm's length from the body. When talking with strangers we will comfortably maintain this distance during a conversation but if someone moves within that boundary we will usually adopt protective postures such as folding our arms, which can be both a signal of defence and a genuine safety precaution. Even in seated conversation we might close ourselves off by crossing our arms and legs.

Is it also possible that we are shielding the chakras most sensitive to emotional and mental vulnerability, namely the sacral and solar plexus chakras?

Displays of emotion can seem to fall somewhere between conscious and subconscious actions. For example, it is fair to say that whilst crying is not necessarily deliberate or consciously driven, it is certainly not something that passes unnoticed by the person shedding the tears. As is the case with most other forms of communication we have a scale of subtlety that ranges from the subliminal signal to the greatest display aimed at the widest audience, and the more sensitive or aware an individual is, the more signals he or she will detect. Tension is a good example; the clenched teeth or tight shoulders of someone under stress can be obvious to one person and pass completely unnoticed by another.

Are psychics more sensitive to the subtle variations and meaning of tension and muscle movement?

## ANIMAL "magic"

Eyes open wide in alarm is a universally recognized reaction. From apes to birds and cats to humans, there is no mistaking the emotion behind the expression. Equally, creases in the brow of many animals can display a wide variety of thoughts and emotions. In humans, the extreme flexibility of the muscles of the forehead enables us to communicate our thoughts in incredibly intricate and expressive ways.

# Astronomical influences

Astrology has long been dismissed by science for several reasons, not least of all the fact that you only have to look at the night sky to see that when astrologers say that a planet is in a particular constellation, they are wrong by one complete zodiacal sign; so can there be any scientific basis for the concept of astrology influencing our lives?

As the earth is not a perfect sphere and has slightly flattened poles, it wobbles as it spins, which has the same effect as the handle of a spinning top moving in small circles opposite to the direction of spin. This effect is called precession and it takes the earth just under 26,000 years to complete one precessional cycle. If you imagine a line pointing out from the earth into space and drawing a circle in the sky, where the north pole now points towards Polaris in the constellation of Ursa Minor, it will gradually move through this circle and the north star will change as the cycle progresses. Half way round in another 13,000 years or so our north star will be Vega in the constellation of Lyra.

Although the origins of the zodiac as we know it are uncertain, it can be reliably traced back to Mesopotamia and certain cultural influences suggest it to be older than that, so the patterns that we know have been part of our culture for at least 5000 years. The gradual precessional shift in the orbit of the earth has meant that it has slipped away from the original alignment, which would explain the discrepancy between astronomical and astrological observations. The only important factor in astrology is the position of the planets in relation to the earth, with the zodiacal constellations forming no more than a background point of reference.

Many people are surprised to learn that the tidal influences of the sun and moon not only pull the oceans but physically distort the solid earth as well. It may seem

astonishing but the surface of the earth itself is constantly rising and falling beneath our feet. Even the gravitational effects of Jupiter on the earth's tides, though small, can be accurately measured and it is through the precise nature of gravity that science is able to detect planets around distant stars. If a star "wobbles" as it spins there must be something close by exerting a gravitational pull, so if whole solar systems and the solid earth can be affected, why not the more malleable creatures who populate its surface?

Another effect of the earth's distortion will be shifts of electrical flow through the earth, and, as the movements of all the planets are known to influence the movement of the sun itself, it follows that the magnetic field of the earth will also be affected. Scientists argue that the forces at work are too small to affect any individual, but as we have seen, tiny changes of electrical flow can and do influence the workings of the body. Could these also have an impact on our natural cycles? If our electrical energy is influenced it could, in turn, affect our chemical balance.

Could this explain why we will be more susceptible to certain influences at different times?

## ANIMAL "magic"

There are numerous examples of animals influenced by the lunar cycle, from howling wolves to spawning coral, and the size of trawler catches is known to fluctuate with the phases of the moon. Research has shown that other characteristics are also affected with one study revealing that the number of people reporting animal bites is double the average daily figure on the day of the full moon. Could the planets also cause these effects on a more subtle level?

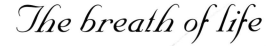

# The breath of life

For now we can only surmise what processes may be involved in psychic phenomena and there is much to learn about the most subtle and sensitive processes within the body. The more we discover, the more things we find in the universe that at first seem to be completely implausible. It is interesting that science now regards time as an illusion; we and all other life on earth have evolved to use time in a particular linear way.

If this concept is correct, is it also possible that, by returning to the quiet space of a meditative state, the psychic is able to step outside the confines of the illusion and access future information?

Along with the importance of quiet stillness, every spiritual background emphasizes the breath as a point of focus, whether it is chanting on the breath, yogic breathing or simply being aware of it flowing into our bodies. Other than the need for air, is there an aspect of breathing that we do not yet fully understand? We have seen that our chemical communications are sensed through our noses so is there more in the air than we know? Of the countless reports of hauntings, many people have described the experience as being accompanied by smells: someone's cigarette smoke, the aroma of cooking or perfume.

Is it possible that, like the sea of energy that surrounds us all the time, we can tune in to past smells or events that have existed in that space, or is it another aspect of seeing through the illusion of time?

There are many instances of people "intuitively" taking a different route while driving and then discovering that they have unconsciously avoided an accident or huge traffic jam.

Is it possible that along with other chemical signals we could, in our breathing, be picking up the increase of stress hormones or even pollution coming from a particular direction?

An astonishing discovery in recent years has been occasions when some transplant patients adopt certain characteristics of their deceased donors. This appears to show that the cells of the body retain more information than expected, which opens up yet more possibilities.

It may be a little unpalatable, but, considering that 70% of house dust is made up of human skin cells, is it possible that we are inhaling more information from each other in this way too?

At the deepest level of physical matter there exist only 92 different atomic elements and everything we know or have ever known is made of a combination of those atoms. Atoms arrange and combine to form molecules, which range from the simplest substances to the most complex, making every rock, liquid, gas, plant and animal; but ultimately they return to their original state time and time again. We are all, quite literally, made of atoms that were once floating in space before the earth was formed. In every breath that we take, we inhale atoms that have been part of everything that has existed on the earth; so on a profound level, just as mystics have stated through the ages, we really are a part of the whole.

And if this is so how might we get in touch with our individual part of the whole? We have discussed the need to be still and to be in touch with the deep part of the self that is within us. It seems likely therefore we need to unfold or peel back the aspects of self that restrict this, and to do this it is thought that one needs to spend time on self discovery. In the next section we begin our journey of psychic and spiritual discovery with simple exercises that show how you too might be able to connect with the deep part of yourself, thereby attuning to the whole energy of life.

# Chapter 3

## Stage one: foundation for spiritual self-development

*The first steps on the path to spiritual self-development are those that enable individuals to be more open to spiritual influences. Exercises in meditation, visualization, accessing subtle energies and connecting with your chakras will assist the process.*

# Meditation

Some form of meditation has been with us throughout history and as we have seen in the previous chapters there are positive reasons for its implementation. Meditation exists in many forms still in common use including repetitive prayer, mantras and chant. Its purpose is to bring your whole energy into a state of stillness so you can be more in touch with what is real and right for you. It helps you to transcend the painful and negative aspects of everyday life and to live with a serenity, an inner peace, and a joy and love of life. It is the search for, and experience of, the relationship of the individual with him- or herself and the attunement to the whole universal energy. It is an alignment of awareness that draws us towards higher spiritual development.

Although many people believe prayer enables them to find solutions, many also advocate a form of "conscious" prayer, which means being aware of the connectedness to the divine. Prayer in its usual mode might be thought of as a request, plea or a form of supplication to God or other deities, whereas meditation is seen as "attunement" or "at-one-ment" to a higher force or God. The terms "prayer" and "meditation" can cause confusion. As the transpersonalist and parapsychologist Charles Tart has written: "Meditation properly refers to internal psychological practices intended to change the quality or state of consciousness of your mind, its efficacy comes exclusively from the meditation. Prayer on the other hand is effective insofar as there is a supernatural or non ordinary order of Being or being who might respond to it."

There is a phrase in the East that talks about the "monkey mind". In meditation we are seeking to quieten this lively and sometimes obstreperous mind. It requires some patience and it's a bit like training a dog to a lead; we are trying to bring our thought process into line and focus. Meditation allows the outer "noise" of the world to subside, which enables contact with the inner or higher soul self. It also enables the person to be focused in the present in a state of mindfulness, which is the ability to observe one's own moment-to-moment changing experience. For the purpose of spiritual self-development, it has much value. It aligns us to the inner core spirit of self, which has the effect of allowing us to feel safe and letting us see ourselves as we truly are.

# Meditation exercises

There is an array of meditation methods including repeating a sound, word or mantra, which enables the mind to come into focus. Some meditation schools will give you your own special sound or word that can be utilized for this purpose. Equally you can create your own. However, if you choose your own word take care that it expresses the energy you truly want.

When you start to meditate it might be quite difficult to just go into stillness and some method or tool can assist you. It's a good idea not to make this too complicated so, if you want an image to use as a focus, choose something that is close at hand such as a flower or a potent picture. A candle can be useful as it is a source of light and we are endeavouring to connect with the light part of ourselves.

One of the simplest tools is our own breathing. Breath, as discussed in chapter two, is a powerful tool and has been used for the purpose of meditation over millennia.

Transpersonal psychology sometimes uses altered states of consciousness as a tool in the psycho-spiritual development process. Meditation is a form of altered consciousness, and it has been found that bringing in these altered states may provide different or even more information for the individual's self-development. Because of the clarity that meditation often brings, it can be thought of as leading us into a higher or better state of awareness. In these higher forms of consciousness there can be a transformation where the usual

**EXPERIENCE**

*"When we started doing meditation in the group it was immense. Suddenly it felt like electricity and it was such a strong feeling, I mean it didn't stay at that sort of illuminating state all the time, but when I was there in that meditative state it was fantastic. It felt really brilliant. To be part of a group where everyone was meditating and having a sort of energetic connection with each other. It was really a very strong feeling."*

**EXPERIENCE**

*"I had an experience within that focused breath which allows me to relax from everything that was going on my head or around me and I found that even if I can just go and do it for five minute a day I was getting a positive experience. It's a very good starting point."*

## Exercise: Connecting to your breath

Close your eyes and be willing to let go of the hustle bustle and irritations of your everyday life. Do not give yourself unrealistic expectations at first, because it is not always the amount of time you spend meditating that matters but the quality of the meditation. Keep trying if you cannot achieve the meditative state at first. Like any skill, gradually over time you will find it becomes easier. To let go of the mundane world some imagery can be helpful so imagine a wonderful brilliant light coming down and massaging and relaxing your whole body. Alternatively, you could use the image of crystal clear water and imagine yourself having a shower, cleansing yourself of all disruptive energy.

Mentally scan the main areas of your body starting with your head and working downward. See the light releasing and relaxing around your head; pay particular attention to areas that tend to hold tension like the jaw and mouth. Release the tongue from the top of your mouth; see the light moving through and around your neck. Release tension in your shoulders and upper arms down to your hands and fingers. Move the light through your torso down through your whole body into your upper legs, feet and toes.

Become fully aware of the natural rhythm of your breath – the relaxing rhythm of breathing in and breathing out. Let your breath be natural – nothing forced or pushed, just the regular natural rhythm. Stay with this concentration for a few minutes and gently let that connectedness to your breath take you deeper into the part of you that is always still: the hub or core of your whole being. Keep the awareness of your breath and consciously breathe into that still place. Gradually, visualize gentle waves of light emanating from your core. Move this still energy outward until it comes out of your body creating a circle of stillness around you, with you and through you. You might like to visualize a golden band of light a few inches away from your body that will serve to hold this stillness. Stay with this as long as you feel comfortable and remind yourself that the stillness is there all the time, if you choose to acknowledge it.

sense of self is expanded. The sense of identity then encompasses more than that of a single isolated human being and with that expanded awareness the individual can connect and identify with universal and cosmic forces. Achieving altered states is thought to give students a different view of themselves and others, and meditation is often the first step. It can be seen as limbering up as you would before any form of exercise.

The goal of many meditation schools is ultimately enlightenment, a perfect wholeness in which we experience opening our hearts to all beings, allowing love and compassion to flow through our lives to everyone without judgment or limitation. To imagine this state is going to come immediately is unrealistic; however, if we achieve it for a few minutes at first, we can then learn to hold some of that energy throughout our day.

### Exercise: Breathing into the heart

Go through the first stage of meditation as described on the previous page. Breathe into the area called the heart, which is placed in the middle of the body slightly above the region of the physical heart. Focus your breaths into this area expanding the heart energy, which is not emotional love but the energy of healing love beyond emotions. Expand the energy with each breath and feel the energy circling out and around you like invisible wings of love. If you wish, you can invite any energies that you feel are unconditional loving ones – an angel, Christ, Buddha or simply the energy of pure light. Hold yourself in this state for a few minutes. When you want to finish, try to bring that energy back into your waking state. Enjoy the healing note of love.

A variation on this is to choose what is called a "centre" word, which is used to impress a positive idea and a loving feeling, such as a flower, love, peace, light, tree, etc. Once you have taken care to choose the word, contemplate it and wait. Gradually some association will come to you. Reflect on whatever comes into your head for a few minutes. This may have some meaning for you, but whatever you feel, return to the centre word again and again. This has the effect of allowing you to train your mind to focus and also may bring some inspiration to allow you to see your life in a different way.

# Visualizations

For the novice deep meditation is not always easy to achieve, so having something to focus on is a helpful start and therefore some forms of visualization can assist you towards greater depth. Visualizations can aid the unfoldment and understanding of self, and can help us connect to aspects of self; the parts of us that "knows" what we are not always able to see or face in waking consciousness. Forms of visualization are increasingly being used in psychotherapy to unlock and then speak to the areas of our unconscious. Here are two very simple visualizations to bring learning of self.

## Exercise: The inner child

After taking yourself through the "connecting with the breath" meditation imagine yourself going into a safe and comfortable room. Into this room invite your inner child. Give attention to the way the child looks and acts and talk to him or her. Give yourself plenty of time and then ask the child what he or she needs and what will make him or her feel safe. When you have done this, embrace the child and feel it melt into your heart.

The child is a personification of that aspect of yourself that feels vulnerable and frightened, so give some thought to what occurred in your meditation and make use of it in your daily life. You also can bring a feeling into this meditation. For instance, if you feel hopeless, abandoned or fearful, you can ask for the hopeless, abandoned or fearful child to come in, take note of its appearance, and again talk to it and find out why it feels that way. At the end embrace it as above.

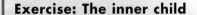

## Exercise: Inner guide

Take yourself through the "connecting with the breath" meditation and when you feel completely relaxed, imagine you are walking out in the sunshine on a day that you have nothing else to do but enjoy yourself. As you walk on you come to a waterfall; you walk into it. Take some time to experience what that feels like and the sense of cleansing your whole self with crystal clear pure water. When you feel cleansed, see yourself come out into a pool of healing waters. Give yourself time to be aware of any images that come into your head, inviting the healing waters to help you work through whatever emerges for you. When you feel ready, imagine yourself sitting in the sunshine and invite a guide or friend to share your feelings and answer any questions that have emerged from your meditation. In this way, the guide or friend acts as a personification of your higher self and you are able to communicate with it, which will assist your learning of deeper aspects of self.

**EXPERIENCE**

"As a drama teacher I utilize both types of mediation for myself and my students. The visualization type can be used to set a meditation off and the purer form, which makes immediate contact with the inner stillness. Although the inner stillness was not there all the time when it happens I often see white and nothing else. I call this being in the whiteness. Nowadays I do not need to use visualization to get into this white open state. I now sit quietly for a few minutes each morning. Sometimes I ask for help if I am worried about anything and visualize light around it, I just send the thought out there, sometimes contacting angels or just allowing it to go into the ether and sometimes although I'm not quite sure what God is I send thoughts to God."

# Subtle energies

It is understood that every living thing is energy and that everything vibrates or emanates an energy field out and around it. It is thought that this life force energy flows through and within every living thing. The idea of subtle energy is found in Eastern medicine, where it is thought that a balance of this life force in the energy field sustains health. While Westeners know it as subtle energy it is also known as:

**Ankh:** ancient Egypt
**Gana:** South America
**Ki:** Japan
**Mana:** Polynesia
**Ntu:** Bantu (S. Africa)
**Pneuma**: ancient Greece
**Prana:** India
**Qi:** (chi) China
**Ruach:** ancient Hebrew.

The energy field is a vibrational energy that interacts with living matter through the chakra system. The seven centres of the chakras (see also next section) provide an emanation or flow of energy that penetrates through the body as though through layers or shells. This substance is called the aura or energy fields. By attuning to the aura, a sensitive person can sense the state of an individual's health, emotions, mind and spirit. Sensitives do this by perceiving the size, shape and quality of the aura, which alters with the physical, emotional and mental states of the person. Attunement to subtle energies also allows us to better understand our own state and what we are personally radiating out to the world.

The subtle body is the non-physical psychic ( i.e. unseen) body that is energetically superimposed upon our physical bodies. It can be measured as electromagnetic force fields that are found within and around all living creatures (see also Chapter 2). These energy fields have been known throughout the centuries and there is a growing movement

## Exercise: Sensing energy

Although traditionally divining or dowsing rods were made from twigs, most commonly hazel or willow, you can turn an ordinary metal coat hanger into a set of rods. Using a pendulum can be just as effective and this also is easily accomplished by finding a strong chain and hanging on it a crystal of your choice. It is understood that thought is also an energy and that thought directs energy. So engage your thought and will to connect your energy to that of the rod and mentally ask for what you are seeking. In the case of sensing the strength of one's aura use the rod or pendulum and work slowly towards each chakra area. You may fine that the pendulum or rod will react to each centre a bit differently and in this way you will be able to ascertain which centre is stronger or weaker than the others. Sensing other people's energies may also give you some idea of your own energy and how it is working for – or against – you.

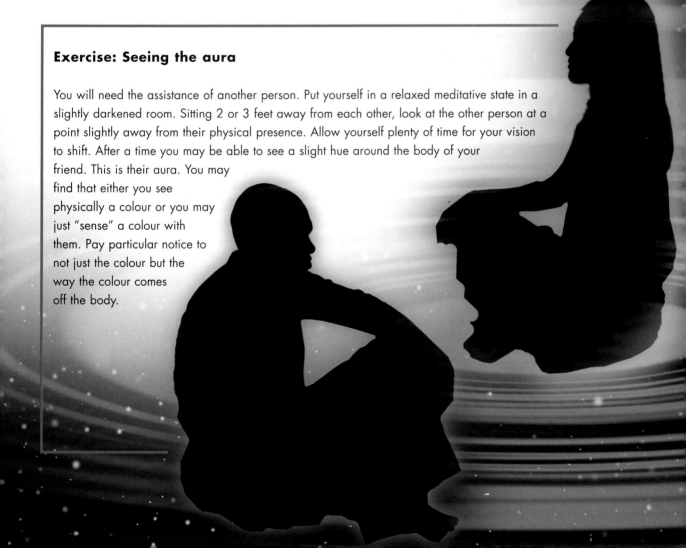

towards investigating how these ancient concepts might connect with modern ideas. Kirlian photography and dowsing are two methods being explored, which might enable us to experience and acknowledge subtle energies. Through these it is possible to see the aura and chakras and work with them to ascertain the health and well being of any individual.

Kirlian photography was discovered by Semion Kirlian in 1940, a Russian foreman who repaired medical equipment. It has been used to photograph the emanations of the subtle body in both plants and animals. Dowsing has been used for thousands of years as a way of finding water and more recently oil. With the use of dowsing rods or sticks you can tune into the vibration of whatever you are seeking, and the rods will vibrate when it is found. The aura or energy fields around the body can be detected with dowsing also.  Overleaf you will find some guidelines to interpret what you may receive.

## Exercise: Seeing the aura

You will need the assistance of another person. Put yourself in a relaxed meditative state in a slightly darkened room. Sitting 2 or 3 feet away from each other, look at the other person at a point slightly away from their physical presence. Allow yourself plenty of time for your vision to shift. After a time you may be able to see a slight hue around the body of your friend. This is their aura. You may find that either you see physically a colour or you may just "sense" a colour with them. Pay particular notice to not just the colour but the way the colour comes off the body.

**Red** Too much red in the aura might mean over exertion. If the red is being thrown off the body it might be indicative of anger. Crimson might mean a high sex drive and scarlet a strong ego.

**Pink** often show unselfishness and sensitivity. If it surrounds the person. it can mean that he or she is receiving spiritual healing or that he or she is a healer.

**Orange** denotes a person of great purpose and creativity. If you see dark or black bits, it could mean self indulgence and a person wrapped up in his or her own emotions. A reddish orange is indicative of someone who is devious. If the orange is being thrown off the body, it denotes sexual desire run riot and might even mean sexual disease or corruption.

**Yellow** is a sign of balanced emotion, clear thought and also compassion. Muddy or dark yellow shows a fearful person who might also be resentful and one that may be lazy and believe that the world owes him or her.

**Gold** indicates a person who is mystical and spiritually advanced. A highly developed intuition is also likely. It is interesting to note that gold is a colour employed by artists in depicting saintly or godly beings.

**Green** Grass green reveals equilibrium and healing qualities, someone who is selfless and adaptable. A soft pastel shade of green might indicate a healer who is connected to the earth. However, any darkness with green indicates selfishness and envy, particularly if it is being thrown off the body. Muddy olive green denotes greed and deceit and can also reveal a depressed person.

**Blue** This usually belongs to someone of an independent spirit who has discovered a way of communicating with divine energies. Often it denotes a devotional or religious nature. It is a healing colour. People with blue in the aura are incorruptible as they have a strength of character that is born out of their inner knowledge. Darkness with blue indicates dogmatism and stubborn qualities.

**Indigo** Colour of spiritual attainment. A seeker of divine truths. It is unusual to see this colour interspersed with darkness but if you do, it might mean that the person is overly concerned with his or her own perfection.

**Purple/Violet** High spiritual attainment.

**Grey/Black** Look at the part of the body where this appears. If it is over the head it could mean negative thoughts. If it is around the solar plexus or lower body, this is someone with negative emotions. If you see dark grey or black enfolding the body, it might mean that this is someone prepared to implement his or her dark ideas of revenge and deceit.

**Brown** is associated with a materially orientated person. Muddy brown might mean someone who is overly engrossed in material accumulation. He or she needs to get what he or she wants immediately.

**Silver** Erratic energy. This is someone with a lot of mental activity. If it covers the body, it might mean mental illness. It can also indicate someone who tends towards an illusionary state.

**White** This is rarely observed over the whole body; if it is, this would be a very enlightened being.

# The chakras

Chakra is a Sanskrit word meaning "wheel" or "disc" and relates to seven vortices of energy, for the reception, assimilation and transmission of life energies. Chakras are a system of spiritual evolution, and their subtle makeup can be explored only through particular means, including meditation, yoga and self-development. In the Indian tradition, the centres are referred to as lotuses: like the flower, we are rooted in the mud and darkness of the depths but ultimately we blossom under the light of the sun. The lotuses are allocated a certain number of petals to each centre, which describes the increased rising of vibration or frequency as one progresses from the lowest to the highest chakra. They also correlate to seven colours

## THE CHAKRAS IN CONNECTION WITH SELF-DEVELOPMENT

| Chakra | Key Aspects | Method | Statement of Intent |
|---|---|---|---|
| Base or *Muladhara* (red) | Survival, physical safety | How to survive in the physical world | I learn through what I have |
| Sacral or *Svadhisthanna* (orange) | Emotions, creativity | How one understands and uses feelings. Creative force and drive | I learn through what I want |
| Solar Plexus or *Manipura* (yellow) | Self worth. The lower mind. Sympathetic connection with others | How we measure ourselves within the community | I learn through what I can and can't do |
| Heart or *Anahata* (green) | Love without judgement. Balance | How to understand and forgive | I learn through love |
| Throat or *Visuddha* (blue) | Spiritual connection. Communication | How to communicate without fear | I learn through communication |
| Brow or *Ajna* (indigo) | Insight. The higher mind | How to perceive higher qualities and potentials | I learn through clear perception and intuition |
| Crown or *Sahasrara* (violet) | Higher consciousness. Depth. Inner knowledge | How to surrender | I learn through knowing |

which the chakras throw off depending upon the speed of their revolution. Colour is light vibrating at different frequencies, and the analogous notion is that as the pure white light of spirit comes down into the physical world it splits like a prism reflecting the colours or energies through the human energy fields, breaking into the corresponding colours of the chakras. There are quite technical aspects to the flow of energy connected to the chakras which are not applicable to this work; however, it is worth noting that it is seen like a current of energy which flows and creates a pattern like the Caduceus or Staff of Hermes symbol of healing. This current of energy is called the *kundalini*. The kundalini concept of the unfolding serpent has long been associated with healing and its Caduceus logo is still used as the symbol for medicine.

Quoting from the yoga teachings, the concept is that we do indeed contain all the higher levels of consciousness as a true potential known in general terms as kundalini energy. This is said to lie dormant, asleep in the unconscious, initially in a state of slumber waiting to rise. Once this dormant kundalini energy is activated, it starts to unwind from the base chakra centre and gradually rises to the spiritual link of the crown centre. It is thought to travel in a figure-of-eight-like manner, rising through the pathways or meridians of energies to which the chakras are connected. This spiraling unfoldment process activates higher and higher areas of self and that movement is thought to change the energy of the individual.

The transformative process creates a series of shifts or initiations until the kundalini reaches the top centre, where connection is made to the highest spiritual energy bringing union to a source or god and a profound consciousness change leading to enlightenment. These qualities or centres connect to the physical by psychic subtle essences or energetic attraction, activated by the life force or "prana", "chi" or "subtle energy". The seven chakras, therefore, could be perceived as stepping stones towards higher consciousness and spiritual integration as the subtle force rises and heightens through each. They also should be regarded as learning tools, intended to enable insight and personal exploration as well as implementing health and healing. In this book I use them as an effective tool for spiritual self exploration through which you can gradually build up strength and achieve transformation to higher states of awareness.

Over the years I have watched the different levels of intuition in operation and linked them to the chakra centres as below.

## LEVELS OF INTUITIVE PERCEPTION

| | | | |
|---|---|---|---|
| 1 | **Base** | Material | Instinctual |
| 2 | **Sacral** | Emotional | Tribal |
| 3 | **Solar Plexus** | Lower mind | Personal, auric |
| 4 | **Heart** | Love | Loving awareness/Balance |
| 5 | **Throat** | Communication | Inspirational/Channelling |
| 6 | **Brow** | Higher mind | Vision |
| 7 | **Crown** | Divinity | Alignment |

1   Instinctual senses are those that put us on our guard from danger, most often equated with an animal sense of knowing.

2   Tribal senses connect with care for our group whether that is family, society or the environment. A sense of knowing what the tribe or family needs or fears.

3   Personal intuition alerts us to people's feelings, thoughts and what they are emitting, i.e. their emotions, thoughts. etc. A sense of sympathy towards others, but also an awareness of fear or threat. A sense of our own self worth.

4   Loving empathy assists any healing process whether in ourself or others. A sense of balance and being able to help or heal.

5   Inspirational links take us towards attunement to unseen forces, a sense of linking to some spiritual entity which is likely to be dictated by the beliefs of the individual, e.g. a Catholic might feel the presence of Mary or Jesus, a Muslim might feel the presence of Allah. These senses also can feel like an angelic presence and may be acknowledged as some form of information, advice or guidance beyond the mundane.

6   Vision gives us a sense of the greater picture beyond selfish personal concerns so that we "see situations beyond the clouds". Exemplars of these traits include the Dalai Lama and Mahatma Gandhi.

7   Alignment to the highest divinity is rare to see, but could be equated to the greatest and best, e.g. Jesus, Buddha, Allah, Yahweh.

# Chakra exercises

Below you will find a useful exercise to awaken your chakras. And because the balance achieved by using the chakras can be so valuable to the unfoldment of self, on the following pages I provide some easy exercises to bring light into every area of life. Although these exercises are fairly simple, the results can be startling. Some latent or hidden issues may emerge; if they do and you find it difficult to manage, please find a competent group or therapist to assist you. Choose wisely as there are a lot of well-meaning people who know very little. It is sometimes the case that a group or person that has the most kudos or is deemed "special" turns out to be superficial and merely flim-flam. No matter how good a practitioner purports to be for some people, he or she may not be the right one for you. Use your intuition to guide you and don't be afraid of walking away if it feels wrong.

## Exercise: Connecting to the chakras

Having gone through the "connecting with the breath" exercise (see page 42), direct your focus into each chakra one by one and simply breathe once, twice or three times into each centre point starting with the base. While you are going through, pay attention to how each centre feels: ask yourself which centres are stronger or weaker than others. Breathe light into each one to expand. The Eastern approach is to see each chakra as a flower; the least petals are in the base, the most petals are in the crown. Visualize each chakra opening up like a blossom. Alternatively, you can use the image of pulling a curtain or opening a door. When you reach the top crown chakra, spend some time acknowledging yourself as a spiritual being.

EXPERIENCE

"The experiential work of the chakras really helped me, it was something I could hold on to and everything started falling into place. Breakthrough came by working with these week by week. I thought, I can see how this works and I can use this to stimulate my intuition so it was a link. I made a link through the imagery and suddenly in a meditation I have a sense of an altered state and I thought 'ah' I know what this is all about now."

Carrying on from this exercise, intuitively choose one of the centres. Whichever centre you choose, focus on that area and see yourself going into the "room" of that centre. Allow your mind to freely envisage the room or place in which you find yourself. Make note of the colours, furniture, pictures or scenery. At some point in the exercise, come into the centre of the room where there are two chairs. Sit down and invite some guide or teacher to speak with you. You can ask questions here. After a few minutes say good-bye to the person and walk out.

If you saw any colours they may relate to the colours of the chakras and indicate something you have to take notice of about yourself. If there was a picture what was it? The picture in this meditation is often an aspect of yourself. If there was any furniture what was inside? Whatever you find there might relate to things you might want to let go of in your life. After each exercise, gently reverse the process and visualize closing the petals on your flower or shutting the curtain or door with the exception of the crown and the base centre, as these are always kept open. Enjoy the sense of peace you will have obtained from this exercise.

**Muladhara**
The Root or Base Chakra

**Colour**
Red

**Location**
Base of Spine

**Area affected**
The bones and lower back

**Quality**
Solidity. Satisfaction in one's existing state and being comfortable

**Energy**
Earth

# The base chakra

The energy of the chakras often feels like a wonderful tree with deep roots into the earth and high branches that reach to the sun. The earth link is in the base centre and the spiritual contact is in the crown. Without the depth of the roots the tree cannot grow tall and so it is with our energies; our roots must be strong and deep. To obtain this depth is called "grounding".

The exercise that follows is very efficacious if you are feeling physically drained, particularly if you do it lying flat on the ground. Directing base energy is also effective for those recovering from operations or even a common cold.

## Exercises
After putting yourself in a meditative state take some focused breaths into the base area. Visualize that energy connecting from the base of your spine through you legs and feet deep into the earth. Not just the surface level of the earth, but where the earth is a volcanic mass of liquid energy. The colour red is very appropriate here; visualize red energy being drawn up into your feet and base centre, which is around the bottom of your spine, just as though you were a tree sucking the energy up from deep within the earth. Allow your mind to focus on any earthy and natural thoughts. As you draw this energy upwards, embrace yourself as a living physical being at one with the earth and the universe.

Finish the exercise as usual bringing back your experience into normal consciousness.

Another very simple way to connect with the base earth energy is by walking, which also can be a form of meditation. Choose somewhere pleasant and walk for at least 20 minutes, two to three

times a week. Get into the rhythm of feeling each step connecting with the earth. If you can find a tree and spend some time sitting with your back against it open to impressions and thoughts, this can open you up to inspirational messages.

Finally, an even quicker way is to stamp your feet around the house and, as you are doing this, really mentally connect to the earth and consciously draw on it. The use of the base enables intuitive connection to our physical needs.

# The sacral chakra

This centre is about creativity and movement and, if it is balanced, is a very powerful tool energetically. It is a bit like an engine or a rocket blast that gets things moving. Many people are frightened of movement and yet our planet is all about change. Indeed, as we speak, our Earth is hurtling across the universe at thousands of miles per hour.

Many cultures have an ethos of change and transformation and deities that personify this. In the Hindu faith, Shiva "the destroyer" breaks down the structure of form to bring change and that change brings transcendence. In Christianity, the crucifixion is about death and yet it encompasses the resurrection that gives us inspiration that life continues. And in all our lives we experience deaths of many kinds – not just physical death but death of childhood, relationships, jobs and situations. Indeed death and rebirth are constant in all areas of our lives. However, with any death comes space for the new.

It is not always easy to acknowledge, but it is often the situations in life that give us most pain and distress, those that make us feel pushed to the extremes, which are the ones that allow us, probably after some struggle, to reach inside ourselves

**Svadhisthanna**
The Sacral Centre

**Colour**
Orange

**Location**
Sacrum on the spine

**Area affected**
Fluid functions, i.e. urine and semen

**Quality**
Creativity and drive

**Energy**
Taste

and engage with a higher aspect of self. When this occurs we almost certainly emerge stronger and wiser and able to move on to greater things. Through the death of our "little self" we can obtain rebirth to higher levels of consciousness.

The expansion of sacral energy allows us to intuitively sense other people's emotions. It is a form of empathy. Unconsciously we are constantly picking up feelings from others; unfortunately, the noise and clutter of the outer world does not always allow us to acknowledge this. Using meditation helps us to become balanced and more aware of ourselves and our needs and the needs and feelings of others. With this information we are better able to understand one another and ourselves and respond with greater affection and truth. Because the sacral centre connects with the emotions it is important that we allow any emotions that surface to emerge and then allow them to pass away. Having a trustworthy person with you is advised.

## Exercises

Having got yourself into a relaxed meditative state, breathe gently and purposefully into the sacral area which is three to four vertebrae above the coccyx, using the colour orange to inspire strength and movement. Visualize yourself on a raft on a river. As the river moves, you acknowledge what you doing when the water is both calm and rough. Go with the movement as the water carries you along. If you are troubled by the choppy waters ask yourself why – still waters are stagnant and stagnancy breeds disease. Without movement your life also will be unhealthy. Consciousness thrives on change and through change we discover new things, our minds expand and we are therefore improved as we explore. It has been said that the greatest thing in man is his curiosity and his need for exploration. It is the food for transformation. Actively allow yourself to be at peace with both the rough waters and calm. Finish the exercise in the usual way.

Other methods of stimulating the sacral are dance, particularly those dances that activate the lower belly like belly dancing.

**Manipura**
The Solar Plexus Centre

**Colour**
Yellow

**Location**
Just above the navel

**Area affected**
Digestive system

**Quality**
Expansiveness, warmth, and joviality

**Energy**
Sight

# The solar plexus chakra

The use of a connection to the solar plexus, like all the chakra energies, instigates change and transformation. In this case, change is connected to will and power. In order to progress spiritual self-development we need to re-define our notion of power to one that empowers and brings strength, as differentiated from the power that takes away another's will. In this work I am dealing with energies. Just as electrical energy requires a wire or channel to direct it, so your power needs direction and will. The transformation of the solar plexus centre emerges from the emotions of "poor little me" to consciously direct your power and energy to make things better. To hold true power we need to embrace our responsibility and take action accordingly. If we let others have their will over us that is equally our responsibility and choice, but if we submit to another without really wanting it, it is not a real energy and it will create problems over time. If we live a lie, however lofty our intentions, that lie energetically disturbs the atmosphere around us and this often has the effect of causing some form of communication breakdown, often with the people concerned not understanding the reason. This is why knowledge of your true feelings, thoughts and aspirations are vital to depth spiritual development.

An example of lack of will is the person who blames others or even life for all his or her woes. Power that is blocked often reveals itself as anger and, when it starts to spill over, it is destructive if it is thrown out on to others. Anger needs to be purged within ourselves and some form of emotional therapy here can be helpful. It is a strange truth, but we are often more frightened of our potential power than we are of our weakness. One possible reason for this is that to embrace true power of alignment to spirit means taking full responsibility for every aspect of our lives. There is an unconscious recognition that this means many changes, which we often resist. Inertia also can be our enemy but on an energetic level all movement is good so the individual needs to engage his or her will and make a move.

## Exercises

In a meditative state, visualize a situation from the past in which you felt out of control or helpless. In your mind, take yourself back to the situation and consciously change the scenario. Do this, not by the enforcement of anger over the other, but by quietly and lovingly stating your wants and needs to the other person or people involved. Observe how you feel and how the other person or people react. Then allow your mind to be unconditionally open to the changed outcomes from their changed attitudes. After finishing this exercise, surround the situation in a circle of light and visualize letting it go into light asking that right be done in the future. Do this without any attachment to any possible outcome.

Laughter is often a good healing medicine for the solar plexus so try to put yourself is environments where there is genuine laughter. Have a small group of people in a circle each laying his or her head on the stomach of another. One person has to say "ha" out loud several times. It won't be long before the whole group is laughing – enjoy the energy of group joy.

**Anahata**
The Heart Centre

**Colour**
Green

**Location**
The level of the
upper breastbone

**Area affected**
Mobility and the heart region

**Quality**
Relationships or sympathy
with others and self

**Energy**
Touch

# The heart chakra

As we come to the heart centre in our development we come to the pivotal point of energy, the bridge between the lower and the higher forces. In the energy of the heart we find the central concepts of most religions and faiths, many of which speak of the necessity to experience and move into the state of unconditional love for real depth transformation. This is present in Christianity as the "sacred heart", in Buddhism as the "middle way" and in the East the notion of "unconditional love". But what does unconditional really mean? Loving without judgment is something very hard for most people to comprehend as we love for all sorts of reasons, many of them to satisfy our own desires, including sexual ones. The love of the heart, however, is beyond personal emotions, wants and needs. It is an openness of love without aspirations for the future. This form of love is not common for even in the love of a mother for a child there can be some personal aspiration and desire.

The unconditional form of selfless love requires some loss of ego and the ability to merge with somebody without any desire of what is required for self. Without really understanding our selves and those hidden repressed unconscious aspects, we can never really get to the point of departure from the mundane to the divine. As we move from the lower chakra energies we can break through to a glimpse of the infinite and a state of love that is removed from attachment. However, unconditional love is not just about loving others; the most important aspect is really loving ourselves including our darker shadow aspect. It is profound love that enables us to accept things as they are; this is not a submission to, but rather an alignment of ourselves to the higher spiritual force of love beyond measure.

## Exercises

Before starting a visualization and after taking yourself into the meditative state, spend some time really focusing on the rhythm of your breath. Breathe deeply a few times then regulate your breathing to be in tune with your heart. Focus your breathing into the heart centre and up to the throat, brow and crown on inhaling, then breathe downwards through the heart into the lower centres to the earth on the exhalation. Do this three times.

Another heart exercise is to visualize someone with whom you are having difficulty. Do this in a dispassionate way without emotions. Breathe into your heart finding a balance of energy and begin to breathe heart energy from you to that person. This might be difficult at first and if you find yourself feeling any kind of animosity stop the exercise and try again later. If you find you are getting emotional it can be helpful to see the other person as a photograph or two-dimensional image. With practice you will be able to allow an outpouring of heart energy to another without any aspirations as to any possible outcomes. This point is very important as unconditional love means without judgment or attachment to outcome. Be honest with yourself. If you succeed, even if it is only for a few seconds, you have probably broken the negativity between you. It's easy to give love to someone we ourselves emotionally love but the love of the heart has no separation and no boundaries.

Often this exercise can really turn a situation or relationship around, but equally if it means that person has to leave our lives, accept this as part of the process of healing and transformation. Working with unconditional love means we can be in an unclouded space intuitively, which allows us to open up to others in a clear and receptive way.

**Visuddha**
The Throat Centre

**Colour**
Blue

**Location**
Around the throat area

**Area affected**
The throat and ears

**Quality**
Communication

**Energy**
Space

# The throat chakra

When we come to the fifth centre, we have crossed the bridge from the lower mundane into the higher realms. This centre opens us up to higher vibrational energy and allows a degree of sensitivity beyond normal every day occurrences. Not surprisingly, the throat centre has a lot to do with communication and sound. Sound is a vibration and can affect us profoundly; it has been used in all cultures as a form of prayer, meditation and celebration of higher forces. Chanting is to be found around the globe and the rhythm of the chant has a peaceful and meditative effect on us. The Hindu term for the throat chakra, *visuddha*, means purification. It suggests that to fully obtain connection and openness, we need to have reached a certain level of purification.

The more subtle levels of the higher centres require greater sensitivity, which is fully in line with the idea that the higher the consciousness, the higher the vibrational note of the individual. Heightened consciousness requires a great deal of dedication and purpose. In reality, there are very few people that can take on this task as it requires scrupulous commitment to the real truth of who you are. Truth has its own clarity and vibrational energy so that when we hear someone speaking right from the heart and core of his or her being, even if we don't necessarily agree with him or her, we tend to listen and respect the individual.

## Exercise

Having opened up in the usual way, pay particular attention to your breathing and try to get the rhythm of it in tune with your heart. The use of sound is extremely helpful here so start by gentle humming. (When you use sound don't allow the sound to get stuck. Feel the vibration before you make a sound and then let it channel from your being.) There are various sounds or mantras that can be effective; the traditional sound for the throat is "Ham". An English version of an appropriate mantra is "I am that I am". This mantra connects the individual with the universal energy. You can say or sing it. Other sounds that are helpful are the "Omm" sound, thought to be the

original sound from which the universe was formed. The Hebrew mantra "Amen" is similar in sound to this.

Listen to the sound you make from within, and don't concern yourself with what it sounds like externally. Chant the sound as many times as you like. In your visualization for this centre, take yourself up into a spacious sky and feel as though you are flying like a bird allowing your senses to be as graphic as they want to be. As you come back onto the ground, visualize a tree with a single bird on a branch and listen to his sound and try to absorb it into your being. Try to hum in tune with the sound you are hearing within, and let the sound float through your throat. When you have finished, visualize a golden cape around your whole body and be particularly aware of the feeling of the earth under your feet. Get up and gently walk around for a minute or two before you get on with you daily life, so you can be sure you are back in your body.

**Ajna**
The Brow Centre

**Colour**
Indigo

**Location**
Slightly above and in-between
the eyebrows

**Area affected**
The eyes and ears

**Quality**
Perceptions beyond
the material

**Energy**
Vision/ Time

# The brow chakra

Opening the brow centre opens a window to what is described as the third eye. You have probably seen the ancient Egyptian motif of the third eye portraying the brow centre. It is synonymous with the true meaning of the word clairvoyant, or clear vision. This is the part of us that "sees" and has vision beyond the mundane. With this centre fully opened, one comes into a vision that has an overview. You see beyond and above what is going on. This view largely ignores detail but gives breadth of understanding that most people never see. The evolution of the individual at this level is someone who is beyond prejudice and sees things as they are and not coloured by what they want. It connects with light. Light is a very fast element and with it we step out of time and space. Light is produced by the excited energy of electrons; as they circle they jump to form a quantum leap. The raised energy from the brow takes us towards a leap of consciousness. This leap somewhat removes us from the material and our vision and view of life can radically alter. The view of a man at the top of the mountain is different to the view of the man at the bottom; they both have their reality and neither are wrong, but if they don't experience it for themselves they may not understand the other's view. Although the brow is a high vibration many people find this centre opens automatically in times of great stress or danger when suddenly they "know" what to do.

A good exercise for this centre is to see a light streaming into your brow from the source of the greatest highest good. Mentally ask for light to penetrate through into your brain to stimulate the creaky doorways of your mind that are not used very much. You don't need to have any images at all although they may spontaneously appear. Just enjoy the sense of connecting with a higher light vibration.

Exercising any muscle requires practice and work; so does exercising the use of the chakras. Don't be put off it you feel you are not succeeding. Although visualizations are a good tool there are some people who are not naturally visual, but will, however, have a "sense" of something, which is just as valuable. Nonetheless, using visual images can help to train and focus energies so do keep trying.

## Exercise

Having opened up in the usual way, focus your energy and attention into the brow just above and between your eyebrows. Focus on your mind as a clear, blank screen and onto that screen bring in an image of anything for which you need to have an answer. Maybe you wish to know something about the state of your health; if so, see your body as a silhouette and allow the images to form within it. You also can do this with an emotional or work situation; however, if you are emotionally attached to the problem, it is much harder to allow the clarity without your expectations and wishes getting in the way.

If you do this for someone else, it is important that he or she has asked you to do it. Making psychic connections with anyone who doesn't know is a bit like opening someone's else post. It is also energetically unsound and in some cases is a form of psychic attack. I will discuss this more later in the book.

**Sahasrova**
The Crown Centre

**Colour**
Violet

**Location**
The crown of the head

**Area affected**
The head

**Quality**
The mystical marriage or union
between the universe and self

**Energy**
Light

# The crown chakra

When the individual comes to the crown he or she is in a state of union or alignment to the spiritual essence of the universe. This is not something many people experience and it could be argued that it is not even conducive to everyday life. This is why people go to monasteries and ashrams to be away from the mundane world and concentrate on their spiritual energy. However, it is possible to manifest this higher consciousness in day-to-day living even if it may not constantly be present. In intuitive terms, the crown chakra is the "knowing" state. This is when one simply knows without the use of reason or rationale. You often hear people say "I knew I should have done this" or "I knew I shouldn't have done that". The task is to be open and free enough to have this knowing more of the time and the trust to act upon it.

Our brains hold billions of interconnected nerve cells and as a mechanism of the mind it is limitless. The stimulation of the crown takes us towards a sense of limitlessness and allows perception of a higher and deeper consciousness. As we move our energy up into each higher chakra we climb in consciousness and our reality shifts with every altered state. On a personal level the crown energy is beyond fear.

The major exercise for this chakra is meditation and subsequently bringing this state into our waking life. This is called "being present" or in a state of full awareness in any situation, place or with any person. Even though for most people this seems out of reach, it can be done in small ways every day. If you remind yourself of the feeling of centredness in the meditational state regularly throughout the day, it can become like an energetic tuning fork that brings your energy into alignment with the higher spiritual vibrations and will allow you to live in the present. Research on the effects of meditation (see also preceding chapter) show that brainwaves change into a state of deep relaxation and oxygen intake and heart rate decrease and this has the effect of putting the body in a state of deep rest.

From this state we move smoothly and we are better able to contact our in(ner) tuition or inner teacher – that part of us that "knows" what to do. All of the meditations in this book will assist the process but perhaps the best ones are those ones that simply connect ourselves with our breath.

## Exercise

As the crown is connected with thought, having put yourself into a meditational state, mentally ask a question; wait and allow the mind to freely get some inspiration. Whatever images or thoughts you have, pick one and ask yourself where it came from. It might have come from the past, but keep following it back and further back to its origin. At some point you may find yourself connected to an infinite source which will give you a sense of a kind of blending with the universal energy. Being in this heightened consciousness does not mean, however, that you will not encounter all the myriad experiences and difficulties that life brings, but it does mean you will be able to come to terms with them with better understanding and hopefully see them all for the potential of growth.

# Chapter 4

## Stage two: unfoldment of the spirit

*Drawing on pyschotherapy, in addition to spiritual and psychic techniques, this chapter offers further exercises that provide the means to enhance intuitive abilities for use in all aspects of life and living.*

# Looking at self

There are many traditions that hold that to be spiritual we just need to connect to God whether that is through a religion or priest. Such spiritual connectedness undoubtedly has a profound effect and inspires, heals and can enlighten, but it also may disregard the personal aspect of self. Like many people before me, in my joy at finding my spiritual connections, I fell into the trap of ignoring unresolved personal issues. I felt so at peace with the timeless reality of my spiritual links that I believed this light would, in time, obliterate all the negative aspects of my being. But life has a way of not letting us forget we are in the material plane. When very difficult issues emerged in my personal life, they made me realize not just the benefit, but often the necessity, of using aspects of psychology to uncover past issues and pain, dissolve unwanted patterns and push through fears. The lower, and often the more noisy aspects of our psychological being, often obscure, veil or even obliterate genuine connection with the inner light. We see only through our eyes, and if those eyes are cloaked with old patterns, shadows and fears, we simply cannot obtain full spiritual integration. Therefore, we must consider the psychological aspects of self.

# The four forces

Psychology has evolved greatly in the last 125 years, and today we recognize four major approaches – The Four Forces.

**First Force** What is now known as the "first force" began in the late 19th century with what is called "behaviourism." This attributes pain to the conditioning people receive, and it attempts to replace negative experiences with more positive ones, unlike spiritual systems, which encourage freedom from all conditioning. All types of psychology have their benefits and certain types of depression can benefit from first-force psychology. However, behaviourism is very limited in its view of the psyche because it concentrates on the outward and observable aspects of self and may not reach the underlying problems.

**Second Force** This is the psychology associated with Freud. It is concerned with a deeper understanding of the psyche. It acknowledges the unconscious part of our self and concentrates upon the emotional pain that occurred in childhood. Because the parents of wounded children are themselves often hurt, they cannot understand or even "see" their child's wounds, so over time the child consequently learns to repress his or her feelings and eventually loses awareness of them. On reaching adulthood, such children often continue to maintain these same defensive attitudes as a form of protection. The remedy is a process of remembering or re-experiencing old pains and working through them. The benefits of this form of therapy are obvious and clearly effective, but again it is not concerned with the deeper spiritual aspect of our being.

**Third Force** Starting around the 1930s, psychologists such as Maslow and Rogers, began to promote "third-force" or humanistic psychology. Maslow's well-known "hierarchy of needs" theory holds that when lower needs are met, space opens up for the individual to take account of his or her potential creativity and self expression. Once the basics are taken care of – we are fed and clothed, for example – higher needs emerge, such as altruism and a deeper understanding of self, and they lead us towards self actualization. Humanistic psychology contends that fear and lack of meaning in an individual's world make him or her avoid reality so that the person's life becomes a false or inauthentic one. People in a state of fear will gravitate to superficial things such as inappropriate relationships, drugs or non-stop entertainment, in fact, anything that prevents them confronting what is really present within.

**Fourth Force** In the 1960s, on the back of much of Maslow's work, "fourth-force" psychology emerged. This looks beyond the personal and thus is known as "transpersonal." The basic notion of transpersonal psychology is to integrate all the aspects of self with past traditions of spiritual wisdom. It takes into account the inner spiritual depth of the individual, and the process by which one connects to it is referred to as "unfoldment." It encapsulates the mystical idea that we are cloaked with veils of illusions – the outer persona – that mask our true inner being. When spiritual development takes place, there is a process of psychological unpeeling, layer by layer, until the deepest core of self is reached.

# Our inner force

In chapter one, I talked about what Maslow described as our inner nature, the core and the real part of ourselves. It is a dynamic force that while apparently silent is all the time trying to drive us like an eternal engine. It is ever-present and although it can be inhibited, it won't go away.

One of the most common experiences I hear from students, especially when they first come into this work, is they feel they are "being pushed" and they do not know what or who is pushing. Often the person tries to ignore or fight it until finally he or she realizes there is something very important to acknowledge. This inner force is also a will-to-health on all levels. If it is frustrated, denied or suppressed, some form of dis-ease occurs. At our inner core is the quest for our true identity.

In transpersonal work, there is the means to uncover this core inner self and many of the exercises are very effective if the individual engages his or her will in the process. Together with this process of unfoldment, you can learn to listen to the inner voice; the in(ner) tuition or teacher. So alongside the transpersonal techniques, you also can employ intuition as a guide or voice, a light that illumines your path to your real self. Strictly speaking, this is a form of psychic energy as it is unseen, but it should not be confused with the psychism of the fortune teller or that which is associated with the "new age". Psychic development of a spiritual nature can be used very effectively to assist the process; unfortunately students, if not properly guided, may be side-tracked into the "wow" and glamour of psychic tricks. Deep intuition has no tricks; it is the most natural part of who we are; it is our inner true nature and to cloud it with trinkets that look like gold but are, in reality, nothing but flimflam at best and actually dangerous at worst, is a very real concern. This is where the student must examine very honestly his or her own integrity.

## Questions to answer honestly

1  Do you want the truth even if it appears less appealing or even if it reveals things about yourself that are shadowy and dark?
2  Are you prepared to take this journey into the unknown whatever you may find?
3  Are you prepared for the possibility of all your constructs, models of life and beliefs changing?

If any of the answers to these are "no", in reality you are unlikely to find your true inner being, and you may not journey very far along the spiritual path. In many ways, no exercise however good can make up for the real determination to the will-to-good, the true, the real self.

# Transpersonal methods

How do we approach the exposure of our deep core spirit in the process of unfoldment? What methods will assist our journey?

Over the last 50 years, psychologists explored this matter and "transpersonal," "psycho-spiritual" or just "spiritual" psychology emerged. Much of what has been written is theory but there is an increasing number of practitioners who are making use of methods that uncover a deeper layer of self. It is suggested that the psychological and the spiritual are interwoven and therefore can't be separated, and it seems that we need to address the whole person as a psycho-spiritual unit. Common methods employed use visualizations and dreams.

When the psycho-spiritual journey begins, it is not uncommon to experience more dreaming than usual. This is thought to be the unconscious mind trying to tell the conscious what it needs to know. Many people make the interpretation of their dreams more complicated than necessary. The unconscious is actually not trying to be mysterious or obscure – it wants you to know the truth. So it uses commonplace things to trigger the answers. Most often in dreams, every living thing, particularly a person, is an aspect of yourself. Even if you dream about someone with whom you went to school 20 years ago and have not thought about since, that person might be representative of a characteristic of yours, which is what the mind is trying to relay. If you have a dream about an aggressive or violent person, for example, he or she is a personification of the violent and aggressive part of yourself. Other aspects of the dream will tell you what is causing the dis-ease of self.

The dream described in the box, opposite, has many possibilities. It may be that the

EXPERIENCE

"I dreamed I was in a small room like a cheap motel with a bed and I was talking to a man who means a great deal to me. Another woman entered the room and he lunged at her legs. I walked out in disgust and got in a brand new car. I could smell the newness of the interior. It was not a flashy car but obviously expensive. It was like a cabin with bold looking instruments. I felt safe. As I was setting off, in my rear view mirror I saw the man was running towards the car. I pressed the button for the electric window to close. He ran up to the window and tried to claw his way in. The dream ended with me having my foot on the accelerator wondering whether to let him in or drive off."

other woman and the man were personified aspects of the woman relating the dream. However, in real life, the woman was involved in a love triangle and decisions were being made so it could be the dreamer was playing out her real-life situation symbolically.

The most important part of this dream is the new car. A car or other vehicle indicates one's own mode of going through life. In this dream it was brand new, indicating that the women is ready to embark on a new life. She felt safe in the dream so, whatever her choice, she has all she needs in her life to be safe.

If the people were aspects of her, then she sees herself as "the loose woman" and the male aspect of herself as weak. However, in both cases the car, her vehicle through life, is safe. It is a very reassuring dream.

# Bias and prejudice

At any moment in time we are the sum total of all our experiences originating from our childhood, society, schooling and, if you believe in such things, your past lives. We all see a world coloured by these experiences; it is unavoidable. Some of these perceptions will be helpful to us as when, for instance, we have been brought up to believe that we must consider others and be kind to our neighbours. However, if we end up only doing things for others to the extent whereby we do not consider ourselves, it becomes counter productive to our spirit and our truth. Part of the unfoldment process, therefore, is to really look at our biases, prejudices and assumptions. This is not as easy as it sounds, as we all would probably like to think we don't have any. But we often inherit the fears of our parents. If they had a bad experience, say with someone from another country or culture, that prejudice may have been passed unconsciously on to us.

Biases, prejudices and assumptions will cloak our true self. It may not be possible to dissolve them completely but by being aware of them we can minimalize any potential problems in the future.

**Bias** Being in favour of one thing person or group in comparison with another. e.g. giving preference or making allowances for a friend or a favourite.

**Prejudice** Preconceived opinion that is not based on reason or experience. Dislike, hostility or unjust behaviour formed on this basis; treatment of a person as inferior or nasty. Conditioning and programming by elders or other members of society against other sections, cultures or groups, e.g. racism.

**Assumption** Accepting something as true or certain with no proof, e.g. assuming a person who is immaculately dressed is happy and well or even that he or she is rich.

### Exercise: Biases

List your biases, prejudices and assumptions. After you have thought about them take them into a meditation and ask for guidance. Ask whether they really assist you today.

**EXPERIENCE**

"I grew up in the 50s and 60s and there was lots of prejudice about people being black, gays, you name it and there was even prejudice about God. I felt all that was not right, I didn't want to listen to it because I thought differently. Consequently, as a child, I put a kind of umbrella around me thinking nothing is going to permeate through. But growing up in a family, going to school, going to work, a lot of prejudice seeped through to my skin and it was almost like trying to turn the Titanic at times. I worked in an area where there was a lot of prejudice and I began to feel inside of me there was something that didn't reconcile itself with the life that I was living. I remember thinking 'This isn't right, I don't know where I'm supposed to be and I don't feel right', but when the rest of the world is telling you 'Well this is the way it is' it was very hard. It took courage to try to change this, particularly in the very institutional organization I worked in; I tried to change it and I worked hard to keep my integrity but eventually I had to leave my career because it was destroying me. I had to get back to my soul and to get back in touch with my true self, into my authentic self, the part of me that has no prejudice. The spiritual work I did allowed me to alter these assumptions; it felt as though I was being reborn. It put me back on the path and it freed me from the negativity of separation between peoples, which in turn allowed me to understand myself."

# Transference: the mirroring of self

The notion of "transference" was introduced by Freud after he noticed that his patients were transferring their own feelings onto him. This concept has now become well known in therapeutic situations. When transference occurs, people unconsciously transfer to the leader, therapist or healer the hurt child part of themselves, also their hidden and repressed feelings about a parent or some

## Exercise: Observing yourself

The art of observation of self is something that is always useful as is the practice of detached loving observation of self. Pay particular attention to those people that frustrate and anger you. Are you reflecting your frustrations on them? When you feel antagonistic to someone ask the difficult questions, "What is the trigger for this? Could it be my own anger, frustration or any other emotion?" Be honest with yourself. You really can turn your life around and work to dissolve problems or actually use them to your benefit, if you know. Try not to be frightened by finding a darker side to yourself; see it as though it is just some unfortunate infection to be cleared. Remember, if infection is not dealt with, it can fester and causes dis-ease. Similarly, your unresolved issues can cause great disturbance to you. Better to have them revealed so that they can be worked through and healed.

other important authority figure from the past. It's a bit like holding up a mirror and transposing the reflection of hidden aspects of self, either negative or positive, onto the other person. However, this doesn't just happen with authority figures; it also can occur all the time in everyday relationships. It is particularly prevalent when individuals project, often unconsciously, unresolved issues onto a "safe" person. Mothers, for instance, are often the targets of anger of their teenage children. Such anger is often a result of the adolescents' fears and uncertainties. It is not dissimilar to the idea of "dumping" stuff onto others.

Have you had a situation when someone accused you of something completely unknown to you? This could well be transference. It also can arise when individuals fear a sudden and/or unexpected situation in their lives; it arises when there is a change from feeling in control of things to losing control of them. The fear, when not identified, is projected onto others. It may have little or nothing to do with the person to whom it is directed. Observing this is not always palatable but can bring about awareness of one's own difficulties. For the purpose of looking at self, the knowledge of this concept is useful to understand what really might be occurring. Transference, therefore, can be put to work and used to motivate learning more about oneself.

# Cutting the ties

At some time or other we all find ourselves in a situation with people who are very difficult. This might occur in your work environment, when you feel you are beating your head against a brick wall and are just not being heard. It might happen in a relationship when you find it very difficult to be yourself without pressure from another. This often happens between parents and children, when the children sense that the parents do not understand or want them to do something that, if the children are honest with themselves, they don't want to do. It also happens in a relationship that is not working out the way you want and this is particularly painful for you to accept or come to terms with. You may feel helpless, unable to move within the situation or with the person concerned. Such situations have the effect of making us feel tied and trapped. We may feel there is simply nothing we can do. It is certainly true you are unable to make another believe or see things your way and, on a spiritual level, you do not really have the right to try: free will is sacrosanct in spiritual law. If you try to alter the will, persuade or cajole another against his or her will, no good can ever come of it and usually what occurs is that the other person just builds up resentment, which at some later time will result in separation and much regret. However, it is not true you can't do anything about it. Energetically you can change the vibration and bring some healthy space between the will of yourself and others. The second quote on page 80 is from a student who found it difficult to be himself.

If you are really going to do this exercise on an unconditional level you must be very firm and resolute with the way in which you implement it. It is important to let go of your own personal will in the process and one of the ways to do this is to intentionally, and with focus, make your energetic links only through the higher consciousness both of yourself and the person or situation you wish to clear. This point is vital and without it nothing will really change.

Although strictly speaking you do not have to be in meditation, it is likely to assist the process.

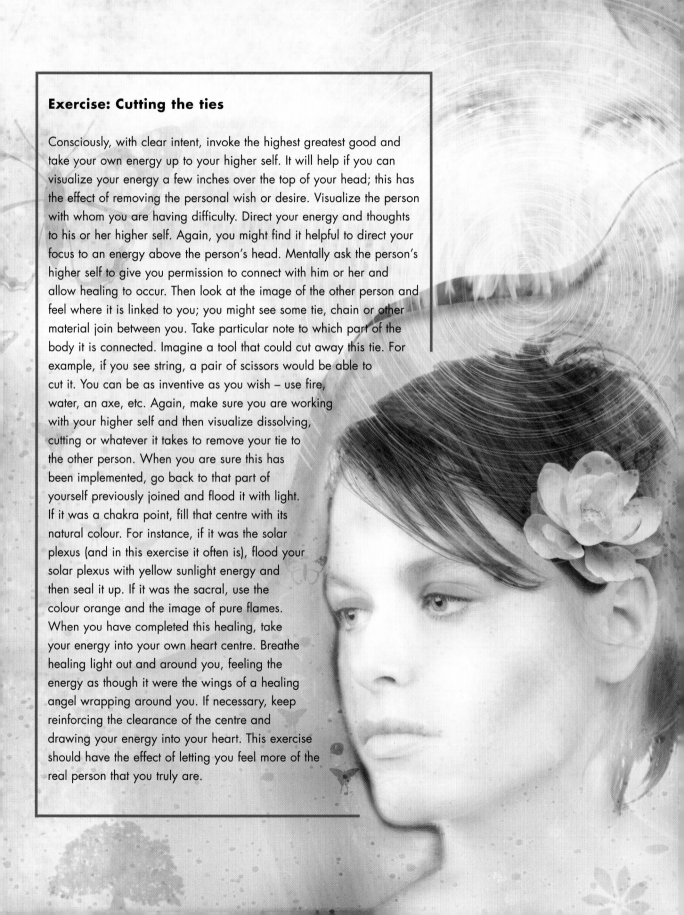

## Exercise: Cutting the ties

Consciously, with clear intent, invoke the highest greatest good and take your own energy up to your higher self. It will help if you can visualize your energy a few inches over the top of your head; this has the effect of removing the personal wish or desire. Visualize the person with whom you are having difficulty. Direct your energy and thoughts to his or her higher self. Again, you might find it helpful to direct your focus to an energy above the person's head. Mentally ask the person's higher self to give you permission to connect with him or her and allow healing to occur. Then look at the image of the other person and feel where it is linked to you; you might see some tie, chain or other material join between you. Take particular note to which part of the body it is connected. Imagine a tool that could cut away this tie. For example, if you see string, a pair of scissors would be able to cut it. You can be as inventive as you wish – use fire, water, an axe, etc. Again, make sure you are working with your higher self and then visualize dissolving, cutting or whatever it takes to remove your tie to the other person. When you are sure this has been implemented, go back to that part of yourself previously joined and flood it with light. If it was a chakra point, fill that centre with its natural colour. For instance, if it was the solar plexus (and in this exercise it often is), flood your solar plexus with yellow sunlight energy and then seal it up. If it was the sacral, use the colour orange and the image of pure flames. When you have completed this healing, take your energy into your own heart centre. Breathe healing light out and around you, feeling the energy as though it were the wings of a healing angel wrapping around you. If necessary, keep reinforcing the clearance of the centre and drawing your energy into your heart. This exercise should have the effect of letting you feel more of the real person that you truly are.

"I was 43 and my mother was phoning me every day telling me what to do. It was really aggravating me. Day by day I just felt increasingly angry. When you suggested using the 'cutting the ties' exercise I didn't want to because I love my mother even though she drives me mad, but something had to change. After I did the exercise, she did not stop phoning me but what happened was I found I simply was no longer affected by her calling. In fact, our relationship has altered and there is more acceptance and we have become more like good friends. I really appreciate that."

"I've been using the 'cutting the ties' exercise on a day-to-day basis as I find I absorb or connect with other people's energies rather easily and find it helpful to quietly just take a step to one side and break down energy connections. I use it as I go through the day if I feel I've meshed too much with somebody else's energy. I have got caught in other people's emotional issues or fear states and I feel like I touch those and feel them resonating within me. I feel that I'm kind of running along in somebody else's tracks rather than my own.

I used to feel that somebody else's thought patterns or emotional patterns had triggered my thought patterns or emotional patterns and I found it troublesome. Now I can simply will myself back, will myself clear again or will my own energy. At work if I'm working with somebody who has a different systems of thought, or emotional belief that is very different from my own I find that there is a gradual erosion of my clarity and I realized that I needed a little quiet time to separate this. Cutting the ties felt like letting daylight in somewhere that had been needing it for a while.

It gave a level of a sense of reconnection. Sense of something that was familiar that had been clouded or closed. I could connect more to the source, to my own place of information and inspiration. I've been somebody who analyzed. I would say too much, now I try not to, I can just say what feels right and my ability to stay in my own energy space increased."

"My next-door neighbours were driving me mad. They were a couple who were both musicians. She practised her piano every day and I could hear it in every room of my house. I love my home but I felt as though I was in prison. I had asked her not to practise and got really angry. She is a concert pianist and she said she had to work. I got very anxious, couldn't concentrate; I didn't want to move but it became intolerable. When I heard about the 'cutting the ties' exercise I felt I would not be able to do it because I was just so angry. I couldn't put it up to a higher source. I didn't feel I could let go of my hostility enough to implement it properly. I thought I might make it worse, but as time went on I just knew I had to do something. I did the exercise although I couldn't hold it for very long. At first nothing happened, she went on playing although I did manage to feel a little bit more relaxed. Then all of a sudden it stopped. I don't know what happened — she was still living there but she did not play anymore. Three months later they moved and I have my own space again. It was miraculous!"

"I have had real problems with two old girlfriends that previously had been very close. It started when my son got really ill and I guess at some point I felt 'needy' towards them and had expectations of these relationships. The pressure was on and it reached a point when it just blew. My poor husband bore the brunt of it. One girlfriend lives in Scotland: I had to wait until last week to see her; it had been over two years. I was really nervous about it and thought I'm ok but I was actually very angry and instead of blowing the anger out on them, which was one way of what I wanted to do, I knew I had to transform that pain into light to let it go and all weekend that's what I have been working with. I could feel the pain, I knew it was stuff that had to be dealt with.

I actually felt that I did transform it last night with the help of my daughter. When I told her 'my solar plexus feels like I've got to work in there', she said, 'Oh mummy what do we do with the stones that we can't lift'? She was just joking and I said 'I don't know', and she said 'We smash them up into little pieces' As she said this I knew she was right and I visualized it; the anger as stones being broken up, and it just went, it just went 'ting' and cleared.

We had a lovely laugh about it and it brought a lot of joy and I felt it. I've been doing 'cutting the ties' exercises; my intent was to clear it and heal it for myself. I also called on angels before I cut the ties and when I saw my friends we all went out for a meal and the kids were there and it was OK, it was fine and I'm sure that what ever will heal.

The main thing I guess that has come out of this, was when I separated from these two girlfriends, I felt that I maintained, created, accepted, opened up to a relationship with a deep spiritual energy and now this is where I take my energies to find inner peace. It was a very traumatic time for me but what occurred was the creation of a profound connection through letting go of my fear."

# Transforming conflicts

As I have described earlier, it is possible to transform and change positively your energies and the way you relate to your world. Not everyone is good at visualizing but everyone has some form of imagination that can be put to good use. Energy follows thought; how you think about yourself and the situations you find yourself in really can make a difference. We all sometimes react to a situation in a way that, upon reflection, is unproductive or even destructive. With practice you can, in a state of awareness, be present in the moment to learn how to respond constructively and not react defensively. "Being present" in the moment comes from meditation and a form of concentration that can be achieved in activities where you have to be totally focused in the now. A tightrope walker, a footballer or a ballet dancer cannot afford to lose concentration for a second. This state is not dissimilar to a form of conscious meditation.

The next exercise can clear and heal a situation after it has happened. As with all the exercises it is important to go into it with a clear and open heart and mind: without that no real healing occurs.

EXPERIENCE

"I walked into the restaurant where I was going to be having dinner with a few friends. When I arrived there was a person I was not expecting and did not know very well. At the time I was a smoker and asked the waiter if it was OK to smoke. He said not at that table but he could move us to a smoking part of the restaurant, I thanked him and asked the group if they minded. The woman who I was not expecting and was not very well known to me was the only one that emphatically said she could not move and was rather dogmatic and stubborn about it. Something about her lack of flexibility just brought anger up in me. What transpired was neither of us would budge and it ended up with me in floods of tears and having dinner at the other end of the restaurant. I realised that it was much less to do with smoking and more to do with my extreme stress at the time and I felt bad about disturbing the evening. Two days later I was able to throw light on the evening and found my friends were able to understand each other better and no hard feeling has been left."

## Exercise: Transform conflict

Often in the heat of the moment our good sense and awareness of self is forgotten. If there has been a situation where you might have felt uncomfortable or irritated and that brought out anger or resentment, and you allowed them to be vented on another person, you can look at how this occurs and move the energy to a different, more productive place. In your mind, go through a situation that was uncomfortable for you. Really be in touch with the feelings you had at the time and recall how you felt and what you said. Remember in some detail what occurred. Try to identify the presence of the person, looking in detail at how he or she was dressed and what he or she looked like. Be in some kind of empathy with how that person was at the time and try to understand why that person reacted in the way he or she did. Keep reviewing the incident imagining being the other person; begin to recreate the situation from his or her perspective. Hold that situation in light. Breathe very purposely into your heart. Then imagine that you were back on that day at the start of the problem and as it unfolds in your mind, consciously change your feeling and reaction to it. Because you "know" a little bit more about the way the other person feels, watch what happens. Change the way you respond. Keep going with unconditional feelings towards the person. When you have brought the situation to a conclusion surround the situation with light. Of course, you cannot literally change what has gone before, but what can occur is that the person with whom you had previously fought may well soften his or her feelings towards you and you are likely to soften your feelings towards the person. If nothing else, you will be more cautious in the future about how you respond in a similar situation.

# Good use of energies

Much of our time, thoughts and energy are spent on issues from the past and anxieties for the future. Consequently we may find that we are wasting energy in areas which we may be unable to change. Although it may not be possible all the time, we can with practice train ourselves to hold our consciousness. This allows us to focus in the moment which is not only energetically sound but also gives us a clearer awareness of our true needs. Being present in awareness then gives us the option to alter anything we wish. Of course it is possible that we may not need or want to change anything but if we keep looking it will reveal what we might best be able to do in order to transform any situation.

EXPERIENCE

"*I realized I was spending most of my days with the pain of a bereavement from a boyfriend leaving me. I really really loved him and thought we were going to be together for the rest of our lives. I spent all my days going over and over in my mind what had occurred. I couldn't understand why this had happened. I was obsessed with it. I then realized I was living with that pain for over 90% of my day. This made me distracted, I was not working properly, my friendships were put under strain and I was tired the whole time. I also realized that all my thoughts would not bring him home. It was hard but gradually every time I thought about it I just sent it into light. Gradually I was able to be in touch with my power and strength came back into my life.*"

## Exercise: Understanding your energy use

After putting yourself in a comfortable space choose any day from the last week. Use your intuition to choose. In your mind, take yourself back to the start of that day. What did you feel when you awoke on that morning? Then take yourself right through the morning of that day. What did you do? What did you think? Where was your energy? Next take yourself back to the afternoon of the same day; go through the same procedure. What were you doing? What were you thinking? Where was your energy? Finally, recall the last part of the day up until the time you went to sleep. What were you doing? What were you thinking? Was that a good use of your time and energy? Now ask yourself what thing or thought took up most of the day and what percentage of time you spent on it. Was it 20% of the day, 80%, or another figure? Breathe into your heart and ask yourself if that was a good use of your energy. If you find that most time was spent on thoughts from the past or with some painful experience, really be very honest and ask if that was productive for you. It might be that it was productive, in which case surround the day in light and breathe back into your heart. However, if you think it was not a good use of your energy, imagine that whatever it was is somehow tied to a part of your body as a wire is linked into the exchange of energy (as connecting plugs were used in old-fashioned telephone exchanges). Ask yourself if you want the drainage of energy to continue. If you know you don't, visualize unplugging from the mains and holding for a moment the plug in your hands. Ask, "What have I learnt from this?" When you feel satisfied with the answer, let the plug dissolve from the part of your body to which it is tied and breathe into your heart centre where it will melt away in light.

# Self identification

Roberto Assagioli saw the higher self as the transpersonal or spiritual self, the "essential beingness." It is not identified with the roles we have in life and is not affected by the conscious experience. The higher self is not the experience but the part of us, the "One" who we are, and, as such, the conscious self is seen to be merely a reflection of the higher self. It is this point that can synthesize the whole being and allow a more essential beingness of human existence. The following exercise originated from Assagioli as a way to be more connected to a real and true inner being.

## Exercise: Acknowledge who you are

Put yourself into a relaxed state. Close your eyes and breathe into your heart. Become aware of your body and how it feels. Pay attention to your bodily sensations. Acknowledge that you have a body and that it serves you every day of your life. It allows you wonderful experiences and you therefore value it. It is a gift. Examine how your body was different when you were a child, the different size and shape it was. Acknowledge it had different sensations when you were younger and also realize it will change as you grow older. It is necessary in the material world to have a vehicle in which to live. That vehicle is your body. Ask yourself "Who is aware? Who has the feelings?" Acknowledge that your health may change. You may be sick or tired but that you, the real you, is not your body.

Next acknowledge your emotions. Become aware of what you are feeling right now. Watch them for a while; acknowledge that they change. Sometimes you feel happy, sometimes you feel angry, the feelings change and they move from joy to sorrow. At times very strong emotions may seem overpowering but acknowledge that even those change in time. Remember, if you can, your emotions as a child. Be aware of how they might have changed. Go deeper within and see that although your emotions may swing from one feeling to another, something within yourself remains the same.

Next look to your mind. Again in an impartial way watch your thoughts. What are you

thinking now? Give yourself some time and watch your thoughts move and change. Think about your thoughts as a child. Are they the same as they are now? Acknowledge that you have a mind and that it is a very valuable tool for expression and for learning. Acknowledge that the contents of it are constantly changing – new ideas, new information. Sometimes your mind is clear; sometimes it is confused. As you observe this make sure you also observe that your thoughts are not you.

In the light of your questions ask again, "Who is aware? Who has feelings? Who has thoughts?" Try to experience yourself beyond the mind, emotion and body at a point of awareness within. Think about the being that is the real part of you that does not

change. If you dis-identify from your body, your mind and feelings, you are left with the essence, the spirit of yourself. State out loud, "I am a centre of being and will, and I am able to do all these things. I am a luminous being, an awareness encased in flesh. I am a being of light; I am a centre of pure consciousness, love and will."

# Round table visualization

There are many ways to access aspects of yourself in order to create a more healthy life. Using an active imagination in the process helps. I end this section with an inventive exercise, which can excite the imagination using the concept of King Arthur's round table. The image of the table is one of safety and can be very productive in finding out more about yourself. Like all these exercises, this one requires you to be honest with yourself. This one can be done on your own and is also very effective if you implement it with the help of someone who has some notion of psychology.

## Exercise: Sit at King Arthur's table

Take yourself into a comfortable place and make yourself as relaxed as you can. It will help if you implement the "connecting with the breath" exercise first (page 42). Close your eyes. Imagine King Arthur's round table. The centre is gold, which represents the heart. Around the table are seated King Arthur and Queen Guenevere and other knights and/or people. King Arthur represents your male side and Queen Guenevere your female, and the others represent additional aspects of yourself. Pay attention to how you feel about these people.

What do the table and its location appear like? If the table is located in an unpleasant place, change it to a more favourable one.

Invite part of yourself to a place where the table is present. The self you invite could be any part of you that you have given up; it could be, for instance, your younger self, playful self, or naughty or creative self. Be as inventive as you wish. The idea at this stage is not for that part of you to come up to the table, it is more just to meet with, and find out what it wants from you. If you have any concerns about the self with whom you are going to work, bring in some help in the form of a friend, a positive person you respect, or a spiritual leader or guide.

As the part of you comes to the place where the table is, take account of how you perceive that part of yourself. Use all your senses – sight, sound, smell, taste, movement and emotion. Thank that part of yourself for coming and ask it, "What do you want?"

If you have chosen an aspect of yourself that feels neglected, it might be angry. It may appear shocked or surprised. Bear in mind that it cannot do anything bad to you because in doing that it would be destroying itself. Sometimes it may appear masked in a nice image, which, when removed, can reveal a very different face. Take account of what is wanted; acknowledge and respond to the need. It may need space, attention or love.

Now request that part of yourself to come to the table and join the rest. If it does not want to come, accept this and remember you can invite it another time. If it does come, watch where it goes. If it leaves, imagine it back. The other self will present you with a gift. Acknowledge the gift and thank your other self. Ask it what the gift means.

Notice if the table or its location has changed. You can continue the exercise inviting other parts of yourself if you wish. When you have finished, breathe the image of the other self into your own heart and breathe the whole image of the people around the table into the golden centre of the table. Dissolve any image and breathe firmly back into your own heart centre.

# King Arthur experiences

The round table exercise can be very powerful and useful. It embraces ideas from psychology and human experience. It is somewhat similar to Gestalt psychology, which concerns itself with the integration of self, seeing the whole being greater than its parts and completing the circle. The idea of parts of yourself being separate is based on people's life experience and Jungian psychology. Jung describes the way we choose to recognize certain core qualities and push the opposites into what is described as the "shadow" or the "dark" side. Unless we are some kind of saint or highly evolved being, all of us will have, to a lesser or greater extent, some darker aspects of self. Nobody really wants to see these and yet do we really want some dark shadow lurking unconsciously sabotaging us or creating difficulties for us? Like a cancer going unnoticed, isn't it better to see it for what it is and therefore be able to cut it out?

Hiding these darker aspects may or may not be intentional; for example, if I want to be recognized for my kindness or courtesy, I may hide my unkindness or discourteous thoughts, feelings or actions. Jung considered the process of what he called mature individuation as accepting the parts of ourselves that assist the transcendence of the ego.

The concept of King Arthur's round table originates in Celtic legend, and therefore is likely to be based on Celtic religious and spiritual tradition. In more recent history, the round table has come to represent democratic leadership as it allows an equal voice. Using this metaphor for integration suggests a holistic process in which all aspects have a part to play. Many people have done this exercise; here are just two people's experiences.

"I called for any destructive part of myself to appear and two youths came and said they were "infanticide" and "patricide." This seemed rather extreme and I questioned it. They certainly did not look like anything that would be so sinister; actually they looked very handsome and appeared really sweet. But then they removed what appeared to be masks, which just peeled off their faces and what was there underneath was horrible and shocking — they looked like demons. One immediately grew and grew, he got really big and overshadowed the whole table. They ran riot, they tried to break up the table and were unruly, aggressive and violent. I was quite scared. I asked them to return to the table; thankfully they did and the golden centre absorbed them. I was quite shaken by the whole experience but actually what I found was that the fear of negative aspects of myself diminished and there was some feeling that whatever dark bits of myself may be lurking I could melt them away and they could never destroy me. The extraordinary thing was the gift they brought was life. So for me there was something about the shadow side being destructive of life itself: like a boil or wound it must be dealt with so it can be healed."

"Ages ago when I did the King Arthur exercise I invited my little hurt bits to the table. Immediately there were hundreds or even thousands of lemmings hurtling onto the table. I did not know what to do so I imagined a hole in the table and invited them to go through it. They disappeared. The gift they gave me was joy. I think this related to my reaction when I feel hurt. 'Cos I do kind of rush at things. I don't mean violently, but I don't take time to really understand and see where I am going. This exercise made me see how destructive that aspect of myself could be."

# Chapter 5

## Stage three: psychic sensitivity

Once the more basic exercises are mastered, more advanced techniques are offered that enable you to progress to learning how to connect and attune with the aura and astral – inspirational and channelling energies that provide a deeper revelation of self.

# Intuition

For the purpose of spiritual self-development we are looking to use a deeper form of intuition to act as a guide, an inner teacher, a directive tool to lead us closer on our pathway to the core, the truth or who we are. Intuition by its nature is a psychic experience. There are different levels of psychic perception and the student needs to distinguish between these to be able to discern the real from the superficial or false. This is a very important factor in understanding what is real. There are many different forms and reasons behind psychic experiences. For instance, a common experience is when we walk into a house or building and feel there is something good or bad. This could be for a number of reasons; it could just be that we are picking up some kind of very different feeling we have never experienced before and this makes us feel on guard or wary, when there may be nothing negative present, or it could be a connection to a discarnate spirit. It could even be a type of psychic memory imprinted in the building. Whatever it is, it is a very different sense to that of a deep inner knowing.

Learning psychic perception is a bit like learning an instrument. It takes time to attune to the very many different energies, to trust your feelings. It requires constant practice and attunement because although people have some psychic faculties naturally, an untrained psychic often does not realise the difference in the levels. This can be misleading at best and dangerous at worst. Most books you read on psychic development only cover the first three levels. These are commonly called the auric levels; the physical, emotional and lower mental (thought level). This means that the untrained psychic usually connects to the lower areas. This can be very helpful, particularly for those people who do not realize what energy, thoughts and emotions they are emanating out to the world. However the problem with this for an untrained psychic is often the hopes and fears of the person are seen as actuality. For instance if someone has just gone for a job interview and they believed it to have gone very well the psychic will pick this up and might say they have got the job. If someone expects a lost love to return the psychic may say your boyfriend is coming back. In either examples this might not actually be the case but only the hopes of the sitter. The nuances of energy are not easy to decipher and, just like learning any instrument, it is only by constant practice and attunement that the psychic can become competent. Also as we have seen in earlier chapters there is the problem of the psychic's own bias and assumptions, not to mention transference, getting in the way. If the psychic has not gone through their own self awareness process they will be unlikely to be conscious of these things affecting the reading. The psychic reading then becomes very unreliable.

# The aura

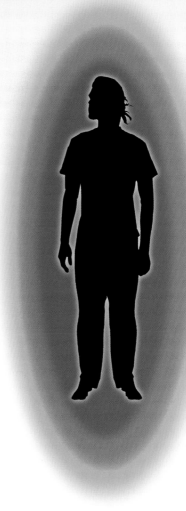

**The lower level** The lower auric levels help us in daily life. On the base instinctive level we may pick up danger, putting us on guard and enabling us to literally get out of the way of harm. Animals in the wild use this level all the time, and it can be just as useful to us. If we meet someone we may pick up they are not to be trusted; alternatively we may psychically pick up they are going to be someone to whom we can go to in times of need.

**The second level** is a psychic awareness of what our tribe or families need. Again this is present in the wild with herding animals. This can be very useful in a work environment when we have to work as a team. On this level we can also pick up emotional energies. We must sense, for instance, when someone is frightened or fearful, we may sense if they are unhappy or if they are fulfilled. This allows us to be good friends with those around us. It gives us the ability to be sensitive and empathetic. This sense is very useful in therapeutic and healing situations; however, although it is good to have a feeling about someone, it is not good to hold on to that feeling. If someone is crying you do little good by crying with them. Many untrained psychics pick up energies from others and find they can get drained. Talking to a friend in trouble on the telephone can do this also, so by the time the phone call is ended they may be feeling much better and

*Many years ago I gave a sitting to a lady who was greatly distressed; she had been to a psychic who had told her that both her daughters would die. Apart from the ethical consideration of such a dreadful thing to say, it was incorrect. This woman's greatest fear was the loss of her daughters; the psychic had picked this up and read it back as an actuality. To someone of a nervous disposition this could cause a great deal of stress.*

you are worn out! Learning to be centred and focused in one's own energy is not just good practice as a psychic but also is profoundly useful to us all in day to day living.

**The third level** is where most psychics get their information. Psychic connection on this level alerts the psychic to the person's thoughts and feelings, their sense of worth and where they are directing their energy. It often comes with images of what is occurring within the life of that individual and it can be amazingly accurate. How that psychic advises on that subject however is fraught with difficulties. If the psychic is not confident and balanced in their energy they may well project their own fears onto the sitter. When I train a student in psychic development I always try to advise the student to say exactly what they receive. If this is an image they must describe the image without putting any interpretation upon it. When this is implemented properly it not only is much more accurate, but it can also cut out the psychic's bias and prejudice of their own feeling around the image.

Individual will can also be a problem in the third level. We all know the feeling of being with someone who is very wilful. Sometimes it can make us feel physically uncomfortable and when it does it is usually felt in the solar plexus area. Energetically the person is draining our energy; however this is rarely anything they are consciously aware of. All the person would know is that he/she feels more empowered whereas the person from whom they are taking the energy feels uncomfortable and sometimes depleted. Linking with this area a psychic can find out what the person fears and hopes but there is a down side of an untrained psychic working on this level. The human emotions are very powerful and this might lead an inexperienced psychic to feel these as predictions. This may not only be incorrect but could be disempowering by allowing the person to think they are absolute. Emotions and thoughts easily can be put across as faits accomplis, not just possibilities.

# Auric exercises

There is no real alternative for learning psychic development other than in a good group. The group dynamics and the evidence and attunement one can receive week after week is irreplaceable. The problem with finding a good teacher is that there are many people with integrity and talent, but unless they have gone through their own unfoldment process they may be incompetent to really understand what is going on with the student. Depth psychic work is not just about evidence, it is about how it is relayed, what quality of energy come through with it and most important of all, how much clarity is in the transmission of the psychic. What has all this got to do with spirituality? The beneficial aspect of sitting in a psychic development group is in understanding another person's feelings, and being

## SIMPLE GUIDELINES FOR WORKING IN A GROUP

1  Use simple uncomplicated meditation exercises like "connecting with the breath" in Chapter 3.
2  Remember it's all right to get things wrong; we all do and only a fool thinks they are right all the time.
3  Learn to listen to members of the group; they all have something to teach you and the one that aggravates you most is the one that you will learn most from.
4  Be humble but don't just be nice for the sake of it: speak your mind with kindness.
5  We are all good souls. People are difficult usually because they are feeling at odds with themselves. People behaving badly are usually ones that have had bad things done to them.
6  Be true to yourself, but don't be afraid to look at the shadow side. Like any infection or cancer it's best to know about it so it can be healed.
7  Trust your own feelings. Be discerning. Usually the most elaborate-sounding evidence or guide is the one most likely to be false. True guidance comes gently with love not glamour.
8  Never be afraid to say NO.
9  Exercises can only work if the person is really engaged into the process.
10  When in doubt go back to the heart. Work with unconditional love.

empathetic and sensitive to others. This serves as a reflection of oneself and most importantly you are likely to receive inspiration for and by yourself which is something that anyone can and does benefit from. Of all the psychic development groups I have led over 25 years probably only 1–2% of participants are working psychics. However the benefit that it has given them in any walk of life is immeasurable. Knowing oneself will lead to being a better person and the process of unmasking oneself takes one deeper and deeper into one's core self towards spiritual attunement.

Unfortunately, often in psychic development groups pettiness and political aspects can creep in. We are all equal in the eyes of God. However, there can be a sense that people in the development groups are vying for being the most enlightened. Who or what can possibly evaluate spirituality? What method would one employ? Good deeds, in themselves, may not necessarily be coming from the heart and if one does something merely to earn "brownie points" the energy is defective and probably no good will come of it. If you are connected to a group where there is backbiting and nastiness I would strongly suggest you vote with your feet and leave. If you really can't find a good group gather about six people together and meet regularly. If there is no one of experience to lead it, run it as a democratic concern. This is a lot harder than it sounds as the simple truth is everyone likes to think he or she knows best.

# Psychic training

When we start working with psychic and intuitive energies, it can be quite a turbulent time for students.

*I had only vague feelings to begin with, which I now can identify as intuition. This was verified by doing simple psychic attunement exercises and allowed me to trust my intuition more and realize I did not necessarily always have to have some rational or logical explanation for things. Sceptics might argue that these experiences might be explained by all manner of things, even eating the right food!*

In other words this student is saying that people might dismiss intuition for a number of seemingly more rational explanations; however, this was "not her explanation."

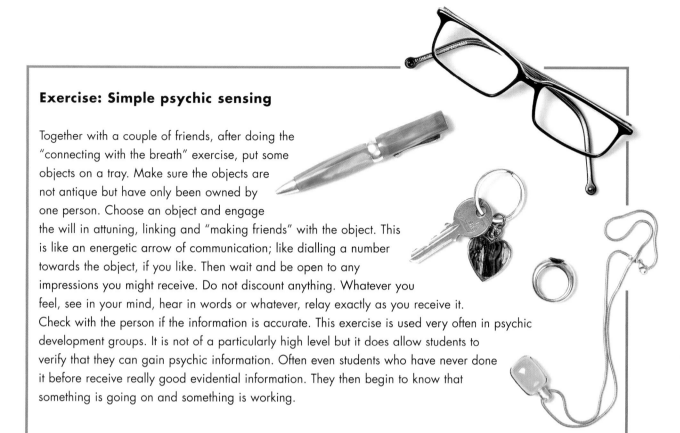

## Exercise: Simple psychic sensing

Together with a couple of friends, after doing the "connecting with the breath" exercise, put some objects on a tray. Make sure the objects are not antique but have only been owned by one person. Choose an object and engage the will in attuning, linking and "making friends" with the object. This is like an energetic arrow of communication; like dialling a number towards the object, if you like. Then wait and be open to any impressions you might receive. Do not discount anything. Whatever you feel, see in your mind, hear in words or whatever, relay exactly as you receive it. Check with the person if the information is accurate. This exercise is used very often in psychic development groups. It is not of a particularly high level but it does allow students to verify that they can gain psychic information. Often even students who have never done it before receive really good evidential information. They then begin to know that something is going on and something is working.

During this period of development there can be a kind of inner tug of war happening. In this particular student's case, it was a fight between her logic and rational thinking and her inner feelings, of which the latter she 'still has allegiance'. The rational mind told her not to continue, but was counterbalanced by her own inner feelings that drew her back week after week. For many weeks she thrashed about with these contra feelings, often requiring discussions after class. Her protestations were listened to and although she was given reassurance that she was all right, the decision to stay or leave was very much put back into her own hands. She describes one of the first exercises she tried:

*I thought this isn't going to work. This is fairground stuff, I thought, this is mumbo jumbo magic and very silly. But I thought well I'm here and I'll have a go and I was scared because… I'm going to fail and I'm not going to be able to do this … I picked up somebody's ring and had all these images and so obviously I was linking to something and thought, oh that's a bit strange, I can do this…this taught me to trust more, go with the flow, not immediately to have a rational explanation, a logical explanation.*

She was initially not sure of anything and she found it all "very difficult" but the fact that she received positive confirmation of her own intuition through the exercises was the major factor to her continuing the development programme and she relays that "deep down I knew there was something in it". At the beginning, she realized that she was "only skimming the surface", "there is obviously a lot more there".

On page 99 you'll find an exercise that is used very often in psychic development groups. It is not of a particularly high level but it does allow students to verify that they can gain psychic information. Often even students who have never done it before receive really good evidential information. They then begin to know that something is going on and something is working.

# *Psychic energy*

As we saw in Chapter 2 there are some scientific explanations of how a psychic picks up energy. One student who is a scientist explains:

*I now understand human beings are energetic creatures in the sense of having electro-magnetic variation waves around and I believe that all thoughts and emotions are stored in their energetic body. I'm not sure whether the use of the word energy is quite correct; it is a misnomer as this may mean something different to physicists. However, we are spiritually energetic and the term is accepted in spiritual and psychic studies so I cannot think of a better one. I now find myself slipping between the accepted rational and energetic approaches quite easily as I feel different senses are used for different tasks.*

There is also a very powerful self awareness aspect to psychic training and one that is not always comfortable. To do these exercises you are put on the spot. You could try and bluff it, but that would not work permanently. The psychic has to be in a silent still space, an open channel to be able to respond to the energies and be an open receiver of information.

*I often felt exposed doing the psychic exercises which was quite hard; I felt vulnerable and they were sometimes frightening. I started feeling people's energies more and feeling people's emotions and feelings and I didn't like it. That was sometimes a bit uncomfortable, I mean it was incredibly useful and I think it's something that I have always been able to do but it was highlighted and I didn't like feeling what people were feeling because it wasn't me ...I was vulnerable, that's what it felt like, being made to feel vulnerable.*

When asked what, if any, value there was in this, she said:

*It gave me another awareness of myself, so in that way it was helpful. I didn't want to be defeated by it ... It was definitely a big challenge to be able to do it.*

She also said that the psychic exercises made her less judgmental.

*Because when we linked with people and said things we must never try and impose things. Whatever you came up with was theirs not yours, so you weren't there to judge and you were never there to say you 'should' do. That was a very difficult lesson for me. I am in a position every day of my life to tell people what to do, not just in terms of the work but in terms of their lives; they bring the most ridiculous things to me and expect me to solve them and just through doing this and also through the discussions I hope I've learnt to do it less, to be able to say this is your journey, even if not in those words. And it was through linking with people and realizing you're linking with something completely different. I got crazy images at first because that's how I worked and the teacher would say 'what do you see?' so I think it taught me a lot.*

Here the student is describing the unpicking of psychic information whereby the student has to say 'exactly what impressions they see without interpreting or judging them '. Students are encouraged to be very succinct, clear and precise. She said she felt this process allowed her to become very much less judgmental in her day to day life. She also learned to use her "intuition differently". It taught her to listen to others particularly in her work as a teacher. She said "you have to listen" and "you have to ask questions, to get them to think for themselves by asking intuitive questions, getting them to use their intuition". She enjoyed the group as she found herself "being good friends with people I would never normally meet" and with whom she would normally have had nothing in common.

# Auras

Every living thing has a field of energy around it called aura. How can we use this to assist our own awareness and possibly help others? You might see healers waving their hands around and wonder what they are doing. They are directing and balancing energy within the aura of the patient, which is thought to have a profound effect on the health of the individual. The aura is not a static energy field, it vibrates and fluctuates as the person's consciousness changes. It can also change more permanently through personal and spiritual growth.

## Exercise: Visualizing the aura

Auras can be photographed as described earlier with Kirlian photography but they can also be drawn. Get a large sheet of paper, preferably cream, and some paint, markers or coloured pencils. Have a subject who will allow you to do this. Try to put yourself in a relaxed or meditative state. Attune your thoughts and energy towards your subject. Draw a rough outline of the body (it doesn't matter if you are not particularly artistic). Around the outline draw three circles, then colour them in any colour that you feel intuitive to use. The inner patch is the physical aspect of the person, next is the emotional and the third is the mental or thought aspects of the self. If you find yourself using different colours in each circle that's fine. Very often we expel a number of different energies at the same time. Look back to Chapter 3 for interpretations of the colours in the auras.

You can also boost or even change your energy, by visualizing light into the area that you feel is unbalanced. Make sure this light energy is not coming from you personally but is coming from a higher spiritual source. Also make sure you are drawing this light in a loving and unconditional manner.

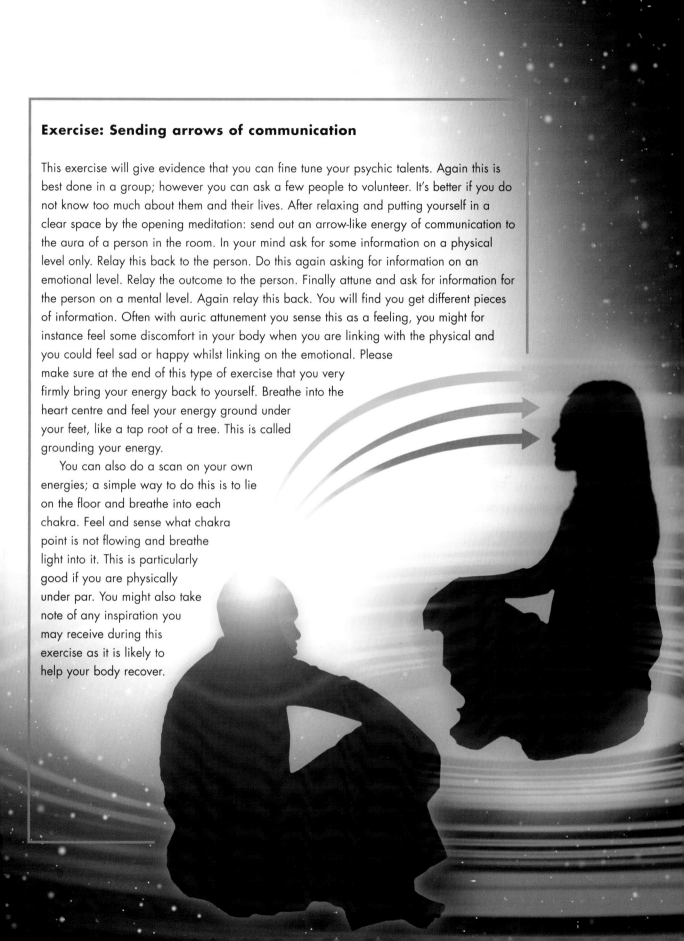

## Exercise: Sending arrows of communication

This exercise will give evidence that you can fine tune your psychic talents. Again this is best done in a group; however you can ask a few people to volunteer. It's better if you do not know too much about them and their lives. After relaxing and putting yourself in a clear space by the opening meditation: send out an arrow-like energy of communication to the aura of a person in the room. In your mind ask for some information on a physical level only. Relay this back to the person. Do this again asking for information on an emotional level. Relay the outcome to the person. Finally attune and ask for information for the person on a mental level. Again relay this back. You will find you get different pieces of information. Often with auric attunement you sense this as a feeling, you might for instance feel some discomfort in your body when you are linking with the physical and you could feel sad or happy whilst linking on the emotional. Please make sure at the end of this type of exercise that you very firmly bring your energy back to yourself. Breathe into the heart centre and feel your energy ground under your feet, like a tap root of a tree. This is called grounding your energy.

You can also do a scan on your own energies; a simple way to do this is to lie on the floor and breathe into each chakra. Feel and sense what chakra point is not flowing and breathe light into it. This is particularly good if you are physically under par. You might also take note of any inspiration you may receive during this exercise as it is likely to help your body recover.

# The tarot

The 22 major arcana, or trumps of the Tarot are not just a fortune-telling device but a powerful description of spiritual transformation, which can help us understand deeper aspects of a our lives and can go some way to enlighten our path. We all encounter many trials and tribulations but every situation can, if probably understood, be turned to our advantage. It is often the very things in life that push our buttons and that we find most hard which are the ones that build up spiritual muscle and in-depth learning.

The whole of Chapter 7 (page 134) is given over to a journey of self, which is described with relevance to the symbolism of the Tarot's major arcana. Though the story is fiction, the characters' experiences are drawn from my many years of listening to thousands of spiritual encounters.

## Exercise: Using the Tarot

Take only the 22 major cards and shuffle, cut and pick the card at the top of the pile. Sit quietly going into meditation and allow the images to take you on your own journey of discovery. Below are three examples of what can be understood.

## HERMIT

There are times in our lives when we have to "go it alone", and yet the card illustrates that we all have an inner light and guide within us. All spiritual aspirants go through some stage of isolation, but this can push us to find some inner quality, some deeper meaning and purpose in life. When this has transpired, great awareness and empowerment occur and we discover a permanent feeling of safety that creates a sense of invincibility which means we will never feel alone again.

*"I had lived all my life on the surface and I came to a point where everything conspired or pushed or I pushed myself to go inward. Something was missing and I realized that actually the inside of myself was extremely important and full of depth and this realization brought tremendous change and personal growth."*

## MAGICIAN

This card talks to us about the power of thought and asks us to look at how and what we think. Muddled thinking creates a muddled life. Focused thought allows us to put out into the atmosphere more positive energy which creates its own magic. Beliefs are not fixed; what we believed as a child changes as we grow and, as we grow spiritually, our beliefs often alter to reveal a different picture. We shape our world through our own notions and beliefs but we can choose to believe whatever we want.

*Intuition cuts through the imagination and it can occur when a person reaches rock bottom and there is an awful turmoil but in that moment there is an awareness and realization occurs. I believe that anything that makes you think beyond where your mindset is stuck assists you because it broadens the way you look at things. So, making me reassess things has actually made me reassess everything — the whole nature of belief if you like.*

## DEATH

This card is often used in films to predict physical death but its true meaning is about death of some aspect of ourselves. Life is full of ebbs and flows and we all experience some form of change or death of situations that perhaps no longer serve us. There is little certainty in life and, as with the seasons, things come and go. Just as spring follows winter the initial menacing idea of death opens us up for new things, new beginnings and better times.

*My world seemed hopeless; I had come to the end of a major chapter in my life. Yet even at that time, I was aware of new growth and movement in the shoots of spring and there was the potential for something more real and important to emerge.*

# Experiences of psychic development

Developing the intuition and psychic faculties as part of a spiritual self-development can be problematic. It is important that the student sees this stage as only part of the journey, not an end in itself. Some students feel it is unnecessary to do psychic exercises, but if they can engage in them they all feel the benefit. Below are some experiences from psychic development students:

> *I started to become aware of people having energy and also that I had energy which I didn't really realize before and then I begun to realize what they were then doing with their energy. It made me feel a bit more withdrawn, because I initially felt very exposed. It made me feel sometimes quite uncomfortable with some kind of new knowledge if you like and I remember I did go through a phase of being quite anti-social, I didn't want to be around lots of people that were you know sort of zapping my energy and I felt quite energetically manipulated because I then started to realize how people were able to drain me if I let them.*

> *We were learning to open the heart, which was quite new. It always felt fantastic to me to actually focus on that part of my being, to be honest and it really had, over a period of time, quite a profound effect on me, you know focusing on your heart and understanding that things worked though the expansion of consciousness though your heart and that was an ongoing process. I understood it mentally, but it took a while for it to actually physically manifest itself; I felt it and it was definitely quite a strong feeling.*

"When I started the classes it was really a very difficult time. I split up from my relationship and I was going through tremendous turmoil and at times felt incredibly depressed and felt really you know on the edge of things, so I think it was a real focus point coming to the class. It enabled me to practice at home. I used to sit down and have time to myself and try to centre myself and that helped me to go through the things I was going through at the time. I used to really like listening to the people I have to say because everyone else's experiences were so interesting and so different and also it was nice to be able in a way to compare yourself with other people because you knew somebody else was feeling similar sort of things then you felt on the right track as well, in a way I needed the sort of reassurance of the group."

"I felt extremely put on the spot and had to deliver so to speak with the psychic exercises and that was really hard and every week we used to talk about it outside the class and think, well it wasn't as bad as we thought this week. I actually felt determined to do it, I really wanted to do it, I knew I could do it. Sometimes I used to think by myself the more fearful it is the better, so I knew that if I pushed through enough fear then it would be really helpful. It seemed to me that I was slowly working through the worst fears in my life. Every fear that I ever had started to come up over a period of years, it was so horrible but actually facing them wasn't as bad as I thought in the end. I felt I needed to pursue things as they came up and I couldn't ignore them, it was so horrible and I wanted to run away, yes I gritted my teeth. But what I gained from it was tremendous ."

# Mediumship and the astral

In the fourth level of psychic attunement we come to mediumship. The word has come to mean different things, but basically it is when a psychic is a medium or channel between the material world and the world of spirit. The psychic is able through this link to communicate with discarnate spirits, guides and teachers. The astral plain is a difficult subject and one on which we cannot delve much here and one might ask why should it even be included in a book about spiritual self development. We do this for a couple of reasons. One is that when students of spiritual development are opening to spiritual truths there is often a period when they are unable to contact their own wisdom direct. When the consciousness of the individual is rising they automatically emanate a call for further knowledge and wisdom.

In the early days it is not always easy to receive spiritual truths clearly. As we saw earlier, often in the beginning of development, the students have more dreams and some of these are not just of the psychological type and there is often a sense that some piece of spiritual knowledge has been received in their sleep, although they may not always be able to relay these in words. In sleep we go into the astral plains and when the students are open to receive, this can act as an open frequency to spiritual inspiration and knowledge.

It is possible to connect with guides through the astral, but whereas this can be inspiring and helpful, one must be very careful because it is very easy to contact a lesser astral energy. On the lower levels of the astral there are many energies that are very good at masquerading as benign beings. Two good ways of identifying these are that they will either give inflated names, such as some known identity: an enlightened being needs no names. Also they will give messages that either inflate the ego or bring fear. For instance they may tell you that you are "special" and have been chosen, or they may say if you don't do a certain thing something awful will happen. Good common sense must be used; remember no divine being will ever tell you what to do. They may advise, guide and heal but they will never abuse the sacrosanct law of free will. That said, a good link to a guiding teacher energy is of extreme value for the student at this stage of development.

Just as there are levels of the chakras there are levels on the astral as well. The lower levels are to be distrusted and ignored. The place that most mediums link to the departed is often referred to as "summerland". This is where you will find a loved one doing the things they most enjoyed in life. For instance if you connect with a relative that loved his garden, the medium will often tell you he or she sees that person in a beautiful garden. If the relative was particularly musical she may have found a place where inspirational music is made. Many creative people feel a connection with this. Composers have been heard to say that they awoke in the morning with a piece of music composed for them in their sleep. Writers talk about muses and inspiration; sometimes they say they feel something else has written it for them. This is a form of channelling and most probably from the astral layers. It's a bit like having access to all radio frequencies and being able to tune into whatever is appropriate. So for spiritual growth it has something to offer us. Be careful though, as it is only one stage of the spiritual journey, a means to an end and not the end in itself.

## Astral attunement for healing

Another good reason for including some astral work in an intuitive spiritual development programme is that it is very hard to get a fix on the energies there. It attunes the psychic sensitivity in a way that no other exercise does. To begin with it can feel very nebulous but as the student progresses they fine tune their connection, and they become discerning and much benefit is to be gained.

When working on the astral level students often have difficulties:

*On this level I never felt strong, it was like something smoky that might be there and might not and I'd try and have a go and it never worked. I accept there are angels and people in spirit but I was not so sure about talking to dead people. The concept was problematic because I was brought up to believe that such practices were wicked and we just weren't meant to do it. I consequently did not fully engage in these exercises and although I felt the presence of my dead father, I would never say I clearly spoke to dead people. Nonetheless, as the classes progressed I lost much of my fear and would be intrigued with what other people said.*

When asked if these concepts had a purpose or if they assisted her at all she said:

*I think anything that makes you think beyond where your mindset is stuck at the moment assists you because it broadens the way you look at things, even if it's only to look at it and then say no. That has to be preferable to not looking at all. So I feel that the whole thing, by confronting me with things and making me reassess things has actually made me reassess other things as well, the whole nature of belief if you like.*

There is another reason for linking to those in spirit that is little used but has some similarity to transpersonal psychology. I have found that putting someone in touch with a relative or friend that they had great difficulties which can bring enormous clearing and healing. The experience below illustrates this.

**EXPERIENCE X**

*One day when I was with my mother when I felt the need to contact my father in spirit. Suddenly he was there and it was so profound. He actually sort of gave me the feeling of so many things that I never experienced with him while he was alive and it was almost as if the whole thing had gone round full circle and he was able to open his heart to me completely which was absolutely fantastic and I never in a million years would have anticipated that would have happened and so on a spiritual level, it was absolutely amazing. Then what happened was my relationships, especially with men, completely changed, and actually I'm now with somebody who is so different from anybody else I've been with before and I felt the whole thing had completely healed and it was an immense realization that actually you can heal very difficult things in your life and they do come right.*

*This connection to spirit had a positive therapeutic element as I was able to be present with the energy and watch it transform. After this experience I felt more open, more loving than I had ever felt before to people and circumstances. It was also an incredible healing for my mother as well because my father was saying things to her also, which she accepted.*

# Channelling in the astral

Channelled material is now accessible in many publications. Astral channelling can be classified usually by the name of the link. Such names as "Seth" "Emmanuel", "White Eagle" etc. are classified as astral as these are entities that come through via a medium. They usually have distinctive names and personalities. Often the information in these kind of material is loving and inspirational and sometimes thought provoking. The best of these are very good and do the job which they have intended, to inspire, heal and help and these types are good introduction to further spiritual knowledge as described earlier. Sometimes the medium is in some kind of trance as in the case of the Seth material. However, trance is very demanding on the medium and it is not necessary. If the psychic or medium works at progressing their level of consciousness they can obtain just as good material, or even better, than through trance. Trance means that the entity completely takes over. This can drain the physical energy of the medium and takes years to completely amalgamate the energy between the medium and the entity. There are various levels of inspiration but everyone can link into some form of inspirational information.

**EXPERIENCE**

*"I was visiting my mother and our conversation shifted to my father's sister, my aunt who lived about 80 miles away. We very rarely discussed her and the conversation got quite intensely detailed about this lady … at one point I stopped and I was aware of my aunt momentarily, I could see her and there was a feeling like a rush of wind around my shoulders, I could feel her, sense her, for about 30 seconds, a very very strong feeling and I was completely unaware of what was going on in the surroundings … the following day I got a telephone call to say my aunt had died unexpectedly at that exact time.*

*This was beyond coincidence as I was not particularly close to this aunt. I believe I had contact with her spirit and this incident encouraged me to investigate and develop my intuitive side and become a competent practitioner as a sensitive healer and medium."*

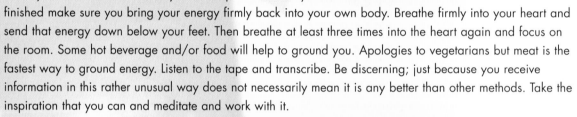

## Exercise: Linking to a higher consciousness

Take some time to go through the "connecting with breath exercise" and any further meditation that puts you in a higher state. Of particular value is working with the heart is unconditional loving energy. Firmly engage your will and send it to the very highest level. Intention is all. Make sure your intention is real. Ask for the highest greatest good, and then go even higher and even higher still, remember there are no limits other than those you put upon yourself. Having sent the arrow message to higher consciousness be open to any information that pops into your head. Speak it out loud. You might wish to use a tape recorder to help because if you are properly linked you are unlikely to remember the words you have spoken. When you have finished make sure you bring your energy firmly back into your own body. Breathe firmly into your heart and send that energy down below your feet. Then breathe at least three times into the heart again and focus on the room. Some hot beverage and/or food will help to ground you. Apologies to vegetarians but meat is the fastest way to ground energy. Listen to the tape and transcribe. Be discerning; just because you receive information in this rather unusual way does not necessarily mean it is any better than other methods. Take the inspiration that you can and meditate and work with it.

The use of an astral link, if it is done with care, is valuable. Refer to the experience of a maths professor on page 111 that led him to develop his intuition.

# *Psychic protection*

There are now many books on the market that refer to psychic protection. Some give elaborate exercises to help build up an energetic layer of protection. Below I will give a few simple examples that are very effective, however please remember nothing can be more effective than you holding a good true open loving heart. This does not mean just being nice to people. Being nice does not always mean you are being honest and there is no spirituality in falseness. In short it simply won't be effective long term. In the next chapter we look at the importance of practising unconditional love and in terms of protection there is nothing better.

The media and films love to present the horrors of psychic attacks. These things are grossly exaggerated and mostly never occur. Most people who think they may be possessed are most likely to be possessed by their own fears. Thought forms can be extremely powerful and if someone is constantly giving energy to some fear or obsession they will over time build up an energy in their aura. This is often seen as some personification: a bad spirit, an unpleasant creature. Nobody needs to have this kind of experience. Bad energy feeds on fear so working to release fear is the most important part of clearing any disturbance.

A good healer can be very efficient in helping in such cases but even the best healer will be unable to completely clear a negative energy if the person is perpetuating it with their own fear. Exercises such as the ones in Chapter 3 will help considerably; here are a couple more.

## Exercise: Encase yourself in a protective circle

Life presents us with all sorts of challenges and sometimes our emotions are our worst enemies. In the work environment, for instance, often a petty quarrel or a feeling of being unappreciated makes life very hard and can build up resentment that is often projected towards one person. In this case do one of the "cutting the ties" exercises. The simplest way to do this is to be in a good space through meditation, see the person concerned and circle them with light. Do this without any preconceived ideas but ask that healing come and watch the person in their circle drift out of view into light.

In a personal relationship you may be feeling very drained, usually this is because there is some emotional connection. It doesn't matter if the person concerned is miles away or even if they are dead. After putting yourself in a good space through meditation, really call up to the highest spiritual light and see that light coming down and around you as a shaft or funnel of light. Fill your whole being with this light and then visualize a brilliant steel tube encircling your aura. Make sure in your visualization that there are no holes in it and it is completely sealed. If in doubt visualize a lock or bolts that keep it fastened. The top is open, giving you access to spiritual light but nothing else can get through. Keep reinforcing this image for at least 5–6 days. You should begin to feel your own strength and energy coming back. If necessary after this time do the visualization again several times.

When there is animosity or even love that is unrequited, there can be a lot of drainage of energy. Although it sounds wonderful to say you have your heart open, when the emotions are involved it is very difficult indeed to reach unconditional love so the steel exercise is a very good one to get you back into your personal energy.

# Chapter 6

## Stage four: integration of self

*This chapter contains exercises for transformative*

*experiences that lead to spiritual self-development and*

*explains how this form of self-development can be merged*

*into the reality of everyday life.*

# Opening your heart

Integral to most faiths and cultures is the notion of arriving at spiritual truths by connection with the heart. Christians talk about the "sacred heart," Buddhists speak of the "middle way" and other Eastern religions refer to "unconditional love." It might seem, therefore, that a similar philosophy runs through all cultures, one balanced through love. If we regard the chakras as a model, we see that the heart centre energy in the centre is the bridge to higher consciousness. Connection on this level can energetically release us from the lower levels that restrict our growth. This concept is central to forgiveness.

Many faiths speak of the necessity to let go, and as the prayer says, "forgive those who have trespassed against us." In many cases, this is not an easy thing to achieve. We are all fuelled by righteous anger at miscarriages of justice that affect us personally. You could argue this is perfectly acceptable, and it is certainly true that for evil to spread often it just needs good men to do nothing. But hanging on to resentment, regrets and anger mostly hurts the person who feels them. It is vital that the individual lets go of lower, unproductive energies. When this happens, I have observed an enormous shift that frees that individual from his or her pain and restriction.

To gain some kind of unconditional acceptance of others requires that you learn to love yourself. This is not the love of ego, or being satisfied with your role in life, job, house or status, but a love that comes from really knowing who you are. Many transpersonal exercises, like the letting go ones in Chapter 4, can be enormously helpful in this process, but nothing can work if the will and intention to look within are not present. Really engage your will in your meditations and contemplations and be connected to wanting the truth whatever that might be. It is like looking in Pandora's box, but I have found that most people, when they do, find that they are not so bad, and any shadow aspects of self can be cleansed and healed if the will is there to do it.

## Exercise: Asking for revelations

Be relaxed, and carry out the "connecting with the breath" meditation. Breathe 1–3 times into each chakra centre, spending some time making sure there is positive balanced energy in all areas. Try, if you can, to consciously align your breath to the breath of the cosmos. Go back to breathing into the heart centre and with each breath imagine healing loving energy flow out and around your body so you feel perfectly safe. Send a powerful energetic call to the highest greatest good and ask that what needs to be revealed to you will be. Hold the meditation for at least 10 minutes. You may not receive any information at the time of the meditation but you will be opening a doorway to greater knowledge and further possibilities. You are likely to get some insight within a couple of days or when you least expect it. It often comes when you are busy with something mundane, like cleaning a floor, driving a car, etc. The mind in that state is often freed and opened to insights.

There is a saying, be careful what you ask for, and it is very true in any energetic work. Here we are asking for revelation about ourselves. This almost certainly won't be what you might think. It will manifest itself in your life and can sometimes come with disruption. However, disruption is part of the clearing process and, in the end, can only be to your good. If your intention is true, you will want to know where there are difficulties whatever they are.

# Mysticism

Contemporary spirituality has concepts in common with mysticism, as do all cultures and religions down the ages. However, like spirituality, the meaning of mysticism often appears confusing. Indeed, the word mystic has, in some circles, come to stand for something nebulous, and is little understood. However, it is generally thought to mean a belief in a personal "union," or "marriage" with a higher source and "being mystical" refers to a transcendence of human understanding. It is thought to be a sense of "connectedness" or "oneness" with a universal force, the living world, God, or "all that is." Mystical experience comes in different types.

**Nature Mysticism:** This refers to a sense of oneness with nature and the living world. It is a sense of immanence – operating and experiencing the wonder of the communication and connectedness within the self.

*When I was in Australia I visited Ayers Rock. I made the most amazing connection with not just the land itself, although that was breathtaking enough, but I also made a link with the history of the rock, the aborigines and their culture. I felt their feelings – it was completely overwhelming. It took me to another place altogether – it was healing and expansive and the connectedness I felt I will never forget. It still inspires me whenever I think about it.*

**Soul Mysticism:** This is the notion that the soul can be put into a state of complete isolation from everything other than itself. It is the quest for right knowledge of oneself.

**God Mysticism:** This is when the inner core self is thought to be assimilated or totally attuned to the essence of the divine so that the individual personality and the world are felt to be dissolved. The soul or spirit is deified without losing its identity by a process that eventually brings transformation of the lower self by the highest self. This process is your own spiritual journey.

## Exercise: Connecting with nature

Gather some objects of nature around you – leaves, stones, fruit, crystals, cones, or anything else from the living world. Spread them out in a comfortable place and put yourself in a relaxed or meditative state, by simply connecting with your breath. Breathe into your heart chakra and move the loving energy outwards and around you, so you feel protective and loved. Take your time doing this. Next, choose one of the objects of nature, pick it up and "make friends with it" that is, make an energetic union with it. Surround and attune with it through the loving energy you have built up. It's important you do not project your own feelings on it, just be open to what the object has to say to you. When you have finished consciously dissolve the link between you and the object. Once you truly connect with any living thing the connection will always be with you, and you may find you want to keep this object and connect with the healing of it at another time. This exercise can give you very different perceptions of energy of the living world and can be done in your own home but even better if you can communicate and attune to any part of nature

# The mystical journey

An age-old phenomenon, the journey of a mystic is present in the Jewish Kabbalah, Sufism, Buddhism and other Eastern religions, and Christianity. It is often referred to as an inner personal journey during which the individual develops and grows by passing through different stages. The story of spiritual development is that of a loving strong inner spirit, which although affected by fear, pain and longing, is never overpowered by these feelings. Its challenge is one of re-vision of life and living. Its process is analogous to that of the matrushka Russian doll – each time you open one there's another inside; all represent the person at different stages.

Models of this journey include that present in the chakra system discussed earlier. The 16th-century nun, Teresa of Avila, spoke of the seven "mansions." The contemporary writer, psychologist and philosophical thinker, Ken Wilber, also gives us a number of models. He sees self travelling as a journey that is taken step by step through the layers as a ladder of self growth. He describes the stages as the "archaeology of spirit" – the more superficial layers of self are peeled off to expose deeper and more profound waves of consciousness. This concept is present in the unfoldment process of spiritual development.

Although the spiritual mystical journey is not always chronological, descriptions of it seem to imply there is some intentionality of self from the individual in the process. St. Teresa suggests that "It is absurd to think that we can enter heaven without first entering our own souls, and without getting to know ourselves and reflecting upon our nature." She, together with

when you are actually outside. If you attempt this, remember to approach the tree, rock or whatever you link to slowly and gently. It has a very subtle and different energy to the ones you are used to, so take your time. Stand away from it and connect before you move towards it, find a place to sit and embrace and merge with the energy. The communication with all aspects of nature can give you healing and a chance to experience different senses.

mystics down the ages, acknowledged that the individual takes an active part and not a submissive role in the process. For St. Teresa and many others, the soul is, in effect, acting as a magnetic force throughout, drawing the individual towards the divine union.

In a recent research study, as I delved deeper into the meaning of these three spiritual models, I was struck by their similarity – particularly between the seven mansions and the seven chakras – even though they are centuries apart. Did St. Teresa have access to knowledge from the East or could these similarities give weight to the notion that there is some immortal universal collective consciousness or a "perennial philosophy" – knowledge across faiths and cultures, and evidence of a possible transcendent unity of religions? Maybe the concept of unconditional love suggests that it is not so much a perennial philosophy but a perennial self that exists within us all.

# Visions and synchronicity

Having obtained some link with the unconditional heart energy brings the student into a very different world and all kinds of possibilities can emerge. However, connecting with the heart rarely comes overnight and even when it comes, is unlikely at first to be constant. The student still needs to be vigilant so that imagination and possibilities do not lead him or her down blind alleys. If, as science tells us, we are all connected with the whole universe, it seems possible to be able to communicate with any aspect of the cosmos. Whereas theoretically this may be true, it can lead the student into cosmic fantasies. The questions that need constantly to be asked are, "Is what I am doing making me a better person now? Is whatever information that is coming to me helping my journey now?" Just as you can attune to auric, astral and higher conscious energies, so, too, can you link to cosmic ones. Whatever the channel or link and however good the medium is, be discerning. It is my experience that spiritual energies encourage, inspire and heal; they do not express anything that creates fear.

In previous books, I have already written (see box) about the inner connection of strength to a spiritual source, which can help you transcend, learn and grow for and by yourself. Depth spiritual knowledge comes in the form of a knowing what to do, what is right and who you are. When you are in a good clear energetic space – being in the zone as it were – and vibrating in a positive sense, often wonderful synchronicities happen. These can feel like a kind of magic. If you think about this energetically, it is because there is a clear flow, an openness to receive. This has the effect of a positive magnetic attraction drawing you towards what you have projected. In this open state, jobs, good situations and helpful people seem to be drawn towards you. For most people, synchronicities won't occur all the time. It is our fears, prejudices, lower wants and desires that get in the way. Sometimes, however, having what seems like a restriction in one's life is also right. So if things are not flowing, have a look; maybe the block is allowing something else to occur, that would not otherwise do so. It might, for instance, be keeping us away from something of which we should not be part. Look deep inside yourself honestly; you will know whether it's better to persist or let go. If you take the analogy of life being like a river and you are in a boat, sometimes the water is gentle and you can lift your oars out and go with the flow, sometimes it is turbulent and you need to row like mad. Knowing when to move and when not and what to say is always a challenge. Do you want to pretend all is well when it's not? Do you want to live a lie? Somewhere deep inside us, we really know the answers.

# Dealing with pain

Spiritual development is full of change, deaths and rebirths. We all, from time to time, particularly through turbulence, experience pain from disappointments, grief, separation, or when our expectations have not been met. When we have physical pain it is usually because something in our physical bodies is out of balance; something is wrong and our pain alerts us to this. Emotional pain is just the same; it alerts us to something being off balance, something that needs to be addressed and, as such, it is not our enemy but the kind of good friend that will tell you the truth. So one effective approach is to make friends with pain, and change your mindset to understand that it is trying to help, not hinder you. Obviously, this is not easy. It might feel that you are making friends with your enemy but often in psycho-spiritual terms, it is your enemy that will teach you more than any other person. To be able to genuinely make friends with pain is to be in an advanced state; most of us would try to push away, ignore or deny such difficult emotions, but denial will ultimately not work as they are likely to reappear over and over until you do something about them. Pain is not something most people can just confront, but any psycho-spiritual work, particularly if it is enforced with unconditional energy, is likely to help.

**EXPERIENCE**

*'Come out' said Lucifer, taunting me. 'Are you afraid of me?' I said nothing but sprang onto him and hit him. He returned my blows a thousand times and lashed out and scorched and slew me which felt like hands of flame. My body just lay there still. But then I sprang upon him again with another body and with another and another. And the bodies which I took on yielded before him and I flung them aside, and the pains which I endured in one body were the powers which I wielded in the next. I grew in strength till at last I stood before him complete, with a body like his own and equal in might, exultant in pride and joy. Only then did he cease and said. 'I love you.' And with these words his form changed and he leaned back and drew me up into the air and floated me over the topmost trees and ocean and around the curve of the moon till we stood again in paradise.*

## Exercise: Passing through your pain

Imagine your pain, fear or anger or any other negative emotion as a person. What would he or she look like? Be very graphic in your descriptions. Give the pain a name or, if you like, simply call it "pain." Draw a picture and write a list of the qualities you perceive the pain to have. Communicate with pain; keep asking why it does the things it does. If, when you do this, you find it hard at first, leave it for a while and come back to it later. Keep a note of it all. If you persevere, gradually pain will explain its purpose and you will embrace it as your friend. When this has occurred, visualize pain dissolving and integrating into yourself.

An analogy from Edward Carpenter, a 19th-century mystic, describing the angel Lucifer is very similar to the process of the transformation of pain. His notion is that Lucifer is actually the angel of light and illumination in disguise, and can assist us if we allow him. In this experience, Lucifer is transformed from being something we fear to something of real value; he becomes a teacher and friend.

# Experiences with higher consciousness

Emotions are often signposts for many aspects that affect our lives; positive emotions aid us in allowing us to feel good about ourselves and enjoy life and living. Negative emotions restrict us; nothing is quite so debilitating as emotions that spill over and cloud our true vision. Learning to deal with them is part of the spiritual self-development process.

*It was an incredible lesson to me that being too emotionally involved with people does not work, even with my daughter. It was incredibly difficult to realise that at the time and you had to let go and then it brought up the questions of what am I doing? And who am I doing it for? I thought that if you have healing or psychic ability or skill then surely you must be able to use it for people that you love the most? Now I realize you have to do it with complete and utter detachment and you can't always do it for the people that are close to you. That realization was hard, I wasn't aware of my own limitation and that's something I'm probably still learning.*

Another profound lesson that needs to be addressed is forgiveness. Many faiths and religions talk about the need to do this. We may think we have forgiven someone but it's not until a situation or circumstance arises that puts it to the test that we really know. Below, a spiritual facilitator decribes a student's reactions in class.

*There was a woman who felt that she had done a lot of work on herself and was vaguely insulted by the idea of looking at herself, but there were so many suppressed feelings and emotions. I think she was challenged by it and was most resistant to going into things like forgiveness and letting go and how that corresponds to an energetic processing. A lot came out. When she eventually started talking about her abuse as a child she said I forgive him but I don't think I want to speak about him or see him again. We were doing something like group healing and she was in tears the whole time and she told the group the whole of this, but she kept saying I forgive him but I don't think I want to speak about him or see him again. So we opened a discussion on what forgiveness really meant and within the process of an hour and a half she went from a point where she said oh you know I've dealt with all of these things to coming to a point at the end where she was basically saying I haven't. So I think it was a very powerful thing and with the help of the group she came to her own conclusion about it because she couldn't hide the fact that it was still so painful. Gradually through the classes she opened up, and was able to let go. She had a serious skin complaint all her life and it all but disappeared and now her whole energy has changed, she even looks different she is very much more free.*

*This episode was beneficial for all the group because it gave a first hand opportunity to look at forgiveness in our life, to question whether we really know what forgiveness is. Listening to others talk and hearing their experiences is a very powerful tool which gives you the permission to look at yourself. People often tell you they know a lot and tell you that they don't need any of this stuff and then learn the hard way that they are not exactly where they think they are. Letting go of pain releases energy and makes profound beneficial changes in one's life.*

# Dark night of the soul 1

If you are still reading this book you must realize by now that spiritual development may sound pretty and blissful but it is actually quite hard work. The process of unfoldment of self allows all sorts of patterns, hurts and pains to emerge so they can be healed:

*Things come up, and looking at oneself so honestly can hurt, but I found once I worked through the hurt bit by bit and again looked at myself unconditionally it worked. I said, "OK, fine that's in the past and next time let's do it differently." Now I have the tools to see things differently and to react differently.*

Because the journey of self is one that has to be experienced in the real world, it is a process that plays itself out over time. Bit by bit, stage by stage, individuals get closer to their cores, real beings and strengths. It would be foolish to suggest this can be done without any disruption and, as one gets deeper, there is often a stage when the journey is very hard indeed. This has been described as "the dark night of the soul." It is often relayed as a form of deep spiritual transformation, which may come with trauma, sacrifice and even martyrdom. When it occurs it could be defined as a profound sense of loss of self; one's ideas, notions and beliefs are shattered. However, it also can mark the beginning of a new life. Old systems and constructs of behaviour break down and you are forced to ask the ultimate questions: "Who am I? Why am I here? Where am I going? And how ought I to live?" This might have the effect of making you feeling naked, unprotected by the roles and masks of the outer world, and all that seemingly protected you in the past.

This age-old question of "Who am I?" is often asked when people are on the verge of investigating their spirituality. One of my students, who had been an enthusiastic student and had progressed well in intuitive development, around the second year began to attend class much less often and when he did come to class, he seemed agitated and angry. Below, he writes of his great difficulty with this process as he, too, had started asking similar questions to those above, about all areas of his life.

I was asking "What was the point of me coming to the groups? What was the point of me doing the job I was doing?" And I also started to wonder, "What was the point of the life I was living?" And I realized these questions led directly to my unease. I couldn't concentrate. I felt like I was drifting and falling asleep and I think now when I look back it was part of the process ... meditation was difficult for me, if you weren't quite focused in intent and there was something about your own energy, it didn't work. It was something like a process going on in my own energy ... I wasn't happy about this and I seemed to be seeing things in terms of getting it right or wrong.

Around this time it began to dawn on me that I was actually uncovering myself. My dilemmas lasted, a long time and I was becoming increasingly uncomfortable with myself. It wasn't very pleasant because it was all about me, wasn't it? I did every possible thing I could to mask it, avoid it whatever, but I now recognise it as a valuable part of my personal process. I learnt it the hard way. I also noticed a lot of changes going on with me physically ... it was a stage that I was unprepared for ... Physically, my body started to come out in different kinds of rashes and things. I became really angry, very irritable and emotionally slapped a lot of people around at the time and I kept blocking it and I realized that something strange was happening. It all built up and finally culminated on a particular day when everything in my life turned upside down in one morning. It was a catalyst point when everything that had built up just came out ... There wasn't any more blocking off to do. I was not in control. I had an inability to hold onto money which was my biggest problem and it had come to the *point of no return on the same day. Also, the relationship just collapsed overnight which was probably the right thing to happen but that wasn't the way I saw it at the time and I realized the reason I was holding on to the relationship was the wrong reason. My world fell apart mentally because that was where I was holding most of these things and things could not have got any lower. All the constructs around me were just wiped. I couldn't physically or mentally cope with that moment so I just had to surrender to it.*

"Masking" and avoiding it, and then finally reaching a break-down point when his world fell apart, is a graphic description suggesting some form of death of self. The student continues:

*Finally, I just sat down and thought I'll ask for some help. I felt that the only way to understand it was to let go. And when I did I had this overwhelming experience of peace and by the evening I felt so balanced and so peaceful. When you let go, all fear evaporates. I just had to surrender to it and when I did that I had this overwhelming experience of peace ... and that for me was quite a turning point ... the most difficult bit was learning to be more of who I am and actually taking away all of those things that I thought were right and weren't. This was a crisis point in my mind, in my fears and they evaporated almost as fast, but at the same time it didn't mean that some of the situations disappeared. And I think that's quite important because many people come looking for solutions to things but the solutions aren't necessarily the way they expect them to be and it doesn't mean that you look at the world really differently but it is different if you feel different or see it differently but actually the same things are happening. It affected me to the very core, but I had a sense that I would have to go through it.*

"All the constructs around me were just wiped," and "it affected me to the very core" are very pertinent descriptions of a dark night of the soul experience, when one's structures of living disappear and there is nothing to hold onto. Finally, as this student experiences, "surrender" to a higher power comes. This form of experience could be seen as a form of death, the death of the past and the self that belonged to it, with no turning back. This death of self process has some correlation to the known phases of bereavement: denial, anger, bargaining, depression, acceptance. His experiences finally led to surrender, which is thought to be necessary for healing to take place.

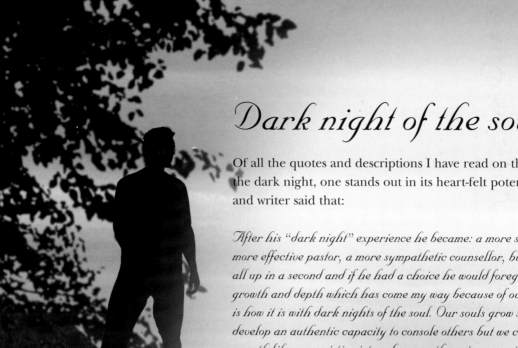

# Dark night of the soul 2

Of all the quotes and descriptions I have read on the experience of the dark night, one stands out in its heart-felt potency. A psychologist and writer said that:

*After his "dark night" experience he became: a more sensitive person, a more effective pastor, a more sympathetic counsellor, but he would give it all up in a second and if he had a choice he would forego all the spiritual growth and depth which has come my way because of our experience. This is how it is with dark nights of the soul. Our souls grow strong and we develop an authentic capacity to console others but we cannot celebrate this growth like an egoistic victory because the price we paid was far too high (Elkins).*

Losing everything that makes sense of your world is very hard and consequently can induce spiritual transformation, but change and death is part of the human condition and to believe otherwise is folly. We so desperately want everything to continue as it is that we have to believe that things will always stay the same. This process has been described as "dying to the self" but it is not really about dying. It is about letting go of all that has held you back. This might mean the actual construction of how you believe life exists. Belief is not set in stone. As children we believe all sorts of things that turn out to be incorrect and as we grow spiritually, our beliefs change, too. But letting go needs to come alongside some connection with a spiritual force whatever name you choose to call it. If there is a connection to spirit, whether this is within self or beyond, it can assist you over the bridge towards self-awareness. But letting go of any aspect of self is not an easy process. Another student explains:

*I think the depth of knowledge gets deeper with the process, almost like an onion, where you keep taking the layers off, and as another layer comes off it's a thicker layer, that's how it feels and so therefore in a way sometimes you think, well hold on a minute, what is it giving to me in my life? I'm not going to know the answer maybe never but invariably the answer as to why I had that lesson will be revealed in my experience. It has been revealed a few times however one is impatient in it, I have been in there in that pain. I do not know the answer as to why I had that lesson but it will be revealed and it is coming much quicker, the answers.*

As described here the peeling of the onion of the outer layers or lower aspect of self can be a painful process and requires confrontation of difficult personal issues.

*I do remember feeling a tremendous amount of fear. I felt I had to confront things and this felt right … I hadn't felt such depth before. Opening the heart felt fantastic to actually focus on that part of my being to be honest and it really had quite a profound effect on me.*

# Transformation 1

Confronting yourself is often seen as part of the self-awareness process and "opening the heart" is an expression that means finding the heart, the core or spirit, the soul of who you are in order to communicate with the authentic self; that part of you that is real, genuine, or pure. To reach the heart level it is thought to be important to be able to transcend at least some fears. The heart level is seen to be the link between the physical and the spiritual worlds and many faiths hold that you cannot journey up to the higher, more spiritual energies without experiencing this heart energy – love beyond judgement and conditions. But it is thought that to arrive at this, one often has to examine oneself, and, as the data and the literature confirm the release of unproductive fears and negativities through this process can be disconcerting. A student relates that in the early part of her development, she was "worried":

*In the beginning, when I didn't have anyone to turn to with the first exercises when I didn't know what was going on, I didn't feel I could talk to anyone, yes that was a worrying time and I thought, in fact I wrote it down; "I think I am going mad," but I was too busy to go mad. It also had another effect when I went through a terrible patch with my husband on the marital side because even that needed looking at but I feel we have come out so much better.*

When constructs change you can feel you are going mad, and, in some cases, change could bring chaos to your personal life. Having a good mentor at this stage is advisable. When asked what made her continue with her development she said:

*I think once I'm in I might as well go through it, that's my attitude, why not look at everything and sort out all the cupboards and see what's there?*

"Sorting out all the cupboards" suggests looking at various aspects of self and once again the need to implement an act of will in the process. To a lesser or greater degree, students passing through depth transformation undergo a similar process:

*It was definitely like an unfolding, so what I was experiencing was then aiding me to unravel things in my life or they unravelled in conjunction with it and that's what I felt. I went though immense changes and ups and downs and bringing up of lots of negativity and all sorts of things happened to me but it was allowing things to process, that's how I felt it.*

Observing negativities and what is described as the shadow side of self is rarely an easy process and takes courage and determination:

*I have to say that the whole thing to me has been an integration so I can't really separate what has happened to me in a way because it just feels that it has all worked in conjunction with everything else. And it didn't always feel like that realistically it's only since I started on this path that everything changed, you know, my path of life, my intentions have changed. They have definitely changed for the better in so many ways.*

# Transformation 2

The extreme aspects of spiritual transformation as in the "dark night of the soul" may be transformative but they can be terrible to live through. Even if it was possible for any practice or teacher to instigate transformation, which is debatable, you would have to question the rationale and explore the minefield of ethical consideration of sending someone down the road of the "dark night" which, historically, has taken mystics close to the edge of sanity. Nonetheless, research suggests that no authentic depth spiritual transformation occurs without change and some dying of self:

*Facing my fears wasn't as bad as I thought in the end and after I got over them I realized it wasn't as though I was being rewarded but what I gained from it was wonderful. And after every set of circumstances something wonderful happened even in my own transformation or events or you know something great happened and I felt like for me anyway I needed to pursue things as they came up and I couldn't not look at them. So when it was a horrible fear, although it was so horrible and I wanted to run away, yes I gritted my teeth.*

Reading this account, it sounds like spiritual development is putting students through a form of torture, but spiritual and mystical literature also imply that any depth spiritual process may necessitate a clearing out that can at times be disorientating. Change is rarely comfortable and can induce anxiety and fear. So the question that emerges is, "Is it possible to minimize this or is it essential to development?"

The effects that spiritual development make in the lived world of each student varies from the heavy "dark night" scenario to the person being able to have a greater sense of self worth. Research reveals that crisis can lead to greater transformation. As one student related earlier, the external aspects of his life did not change, but the response to them did. Nonetheless, the data generally reveals that

changing perspectives can upset life considerably and can upset a student's equilibrium. Spiritual self-development seeks to help the individual obtain a better life, mind, body and spirit, but change often comes at a personal price that for some is just too high to pay.

Spiritual emancipation is something each individual has to see in his or her own way. Each person is different; each has a world made up by different experiences and coloured by many personal elements such as family influences and genetic inheritances. This means every individual will have unique components to look at within his or her life, with different things to transform. Transformation can be achieved only by the individual sensing and feeling his or her way through the process. Intention, engagement, purpose and will are essential; this is not a passive development and it takes time. Some are impatient:

*Well I suppose that's what I've been trying to do but it, took me years and years and years just to get to ... Just to sometimes make a phone call takes me years literally. With a fear of something, it's difficult to let go of traumas because when fear is linked with a trauma it's just very hard.*

# Transformation 3

All the elements seem daunting, so the question arises, "What could counteract these difficulties?" It has been suggested that a real sense of connectedness between the self and a higher force is necessary to be able to come through this process. This connection sometimes comes in the form of awe. Awe is the opposite of fear because in fear we desert ourselves. Awe enables us to transcend ourselves through what is known in mystical terms as "surrender" or letting go. When this occurs, fear cannot touch you. In that sense of wonder, you may be able to set aside your need for certainty. At some stage of your journey you need to feel safe without certain knowledge and to feel safe with whatever happens, wherever you go or with whomever you may be.

If you consider awe to be reverential wonder and profound respect, an inspirational experience usually related to some religious or spiritual experience, it could be said that the opening to a higher power could lead one to surrender to higher forces which, in turn, might to some extent, at least, transform the life of the individual.

There are many descriptions of awe leading to transformation of self in varying degrees. However, no programme is likely to be able to contrive the experience of awe in an actual lived experience. Nonetheless, it may be able to facilitate the opening up of the individual for this experience to occur, and some of the comments concerning meditative exercises seem to show this is true.

As a facilitator of spiritual groups I know only too well how easy it is to get a group of people into a state of bliss, however this is usually of an astral type. A large group of people together often indulge in a mass reaction. Something takes over. We can see this in football crowds and concert audiences, and the reaction can be pleasant or sometimes it can turn to violence.

A powerful orator can instigate bliss quite easily. But the trouble with this form of bliss is that it will not last and the student needs to return again and again to receive a "top up." True bliss is very personal; it is not incited by a charismatic preacher or leader but from a deep meaningful connection between the self and spirit. So any experiential group leader must be mindful of this. The leader must realize that he or she cannot facilitate a personal connection for others. A leader can prepare the ground for the seeds of spiritual alignment but it can only be the individual who does it for him- or herself.

Many exercises will assist the process but an exercise in itself is not the answer. It is how it is implemented and what energy is used. There is no more powerful energy than the energy of intent to good, intent to truth, intent to what is really right. This is how it is with depth spiritual connection. There can be no conditions, no judgement of others and of self. This is not an easy place to be. Very often you might think you are there but only experiences as they unfold will really let you know whether this is the truth. Through depth intuition you can know what to do, what is right, and then you must accept what occurs and work with it. All paths lead home eventually and through your own unique experiences you come to realization and ultimately enlightenment.

# Chapter 7

## The self and Tarot revealed

*In this last chapter I use archetypes to bring alive a story of development. The story is fiction; however, the characters' experiences are ones that I have encountered in my work time and time again. I hope you find it readable and it helps you understand that your spiritual processes are unique to you and yet you are not alone on your journey.*

## THE FOOL

Life is said to be a journey of self discovery. I was young and the world was all there ahead of me. I felt enthusiastic and had no fear of what might occur. I had energy and youth. I did not even take the time to think about my actions or even know I should. I wanted adventure, I wanted to explore, I climbed high mountains dived in the sea and did many reckless things. I had many girlfriends; some I loved with a small l. I wanted variety; I wanted change and adventure. Nothing seemed barred from me.

My name is Chris and I believed I was the nicest person I had met, but then I was young. I had little experience of life. As a child I had a sense of presence; something with me, I couldn't say what it was. I felt I was not alone and that there was some power beyond myself. God was on my side but I did not think too much about God in those days. Sometimes I would pontificate to friends about religions and the violence that they have caused around the world. Sometimes we would talk about different beliefs and that some people needed theirs and it was right to accept different faiths. At that stage I did not believe much at all, although when I was a boy, I sang in the choir and went to church. The only time I attend church now is for weddings and funerals. I liked the singing, but the priests seemed somehow removed from the world and seemed to have nothing much to do with the life I was living. In fact, I suspected they would have been horrified if they knew what I got up to. Like most boys of my time I dabbled in drugs, drank too much, sometimes got into a few scraps, but I always thought I would be ok. Death and tragedy had not hit me then. I took risks with most things, even my

*A fool doth think he is wise but the wise man knows himself to be a fool*

Shakespeare, *As You Like It*

own life at times. I had fun but strangely everything I did quickly became tedious. I was acting the fool and there was not much evidence of wisdom. In this stage of the spiritual journey, one is barely conscious, a spiritual baby where every new thing is amazing. We dive into life without a care. No deeper meanings clutter our world. We have no boundaries; we just live.

I drove too fast and I crashed my car a couple of times but that did not seem to stop me.

On one occasion I went sky diving and jumped over the cliffs. I hadn't really had enough training and the equipment was faulty. I must have had a very busy guardian angle on that day because somehow I landed, albeit with a bump. I was bruised and had broken a leg, which meant I had to be confined. I made the best of it. It was at this time an aunt who was staying with us left a book. In boredom one day I picked it up. I read it, unprepared for the contents. It was a metaphysical theosophical book about an initiate, a wise teacher who lived in the world affecting everyone's life just by being there. It touched on philosophies I had never known although, as I read about them, they seemed strangely familiar. I suppose you could say it changed my life. My leg healed and life went on but my life was never really quite the same again.

## THE MAGICIAN

I was bright at school; I did only the work I really had to and somehow managed to get through college. I was an entrepreneurial type, excited by the kill of getting new business. I made money but spent it. Never saved but always seemed to just have enough for what I wanted. Around my early twenties I craved something big. I needed a challenge. It was the 80s with the money-making culture in full swing, and there was a feeling you could obtain anything you wanted. I set up my own business and worked hard and long. It paid off in material terms and I hardly had time to spend the money that accrued in the bank. On the occasions I went out I drank far too much and there was always another pretty girl that took my fancy. Mostly the girls were one-night stands.

*When to the sessions of sweet silent thought I summon up remembrance of things past, I sigh the lack of many a thing I sought, with old woes new wail my dear time's waste*

Shakespeare, Sonnet 30

At this stage of the journey we are excited by the mind; thoughts and ideas abound. We think we can make magic but the magic we make may turn out to be an illusion if we haven't discovered the true magic of life, the spirit, the core, the truth. I was full of tricks in the disguise of negotiation. I noticed my intuition was extremely good in business and I was able to make instinctive decisions that always seemed somehow to pay off. I never doubted these and looking back I was incredibly arrogant; it never occurred to me I would not get what I wanted as mostly I did.

In many ways I was more alive than I would ever be. I felt in control of my destiny but could not have told you what that was. Many times all sorts of wonderful synchronicities happened; it almost seemed that all I had to do was think of something, make a phone call, and it started to manifest. Useful people seemed to come my way in the strangest of situations; in fact, everything seemed to fall into place so much I began to feel invincible. In a very short space of time I made a million. I had a fast car, I bought fashionable property in London, and when I had the time, I went to high-class clubs.

There was nothing to indicate that anything in my life was wrong, but one day, sitting and thinking about my life, I had the overwhelming feeling I was lost. I analyzed this. I had many possessions. I was certainly successful in a material sense and yet there was an emptiness that once identified simply would not leave. I did not realize it at the time but I was in some kind of spiritual void. It wasn't that I was lonely but I felt very alone. There was a hole inside me that I felt unable to fill. Something was missing. The ability to obtain what I thought I wanted was losing its appeal. The thrill of the kill was subsiding.

It was at this time that I began to investigate a deeper meaning to life. I looked at some of the many workshops flooding the scene. I found a group of people that seemed sincere; they needed someone with financial acumen so I offered my services and started involving myself in the promotion of a spiritual way of life, doing good by making money for spirit, but I knew deep down there was still something missing.

## THE EMPRESS

I watched her out of my window; I saw her get out of her car and go into a neighbour's house. There was something about her, the way she moved. I wondered whom she was visiting. Lucky guy I thought with a girlfriend like that. I saw her a few times and then on one occasion I was getting out of my car as she walked up the road. I smiled, it was a sunny day. "Lovely day" I said. I stopped to talk to her but she was in a rush, she seemed sad. "My father is very ill; I visit him a lot these days." "I know, I have watched you", I replied. She looked surprised. "Oh good", I thought, "she is not visiting a boyfriend." "Would you like a drink some time?" My whole life depended on the answer and some deep intuition in me knew it. "That would be lovely". Before the week was over I was completely in love with Jane. We were close friends from the start and I loved to watch her face as it moved in such expressive ways. It felt safe, wonderfully right and I knew I had met the woman who I wanted to be my wife and who I would love for all my life. I believed I had at last found what would fill the emptiness in me.

Less than 18 months later we were married. I spent my days doing anything and everything to please her. Her face would light up; it made me feel alive, it gave me a special kind of purpose that I had never felt. The day our first child was born was amazing. I looked at Jane in the hospital bed holding our child and I could not express my feelings towards her. She was a great mother right from the start and those days of our children's childhood were so comfortable. We would go on all the outings, take them to shows, make them laugh. What is ever better than a child's laugh – so spontaneous, so natural, so real. Jane was feisty and could just make things happen, we both could. The spiritual group grew and became well known. Jane was intuitive and had caring, healing gifts. When the kids permitted it we went to meditation meetings together. On occasions when she was practising healing, I felt such profound love coming from her energy. My God I loved that woman.

*A child of our grandmother Eve, a female, or for thy more sweet understanding a woman*

Shakespeare, *Loves Labours Lost*

Jane was hugely protective about our two children; she always put them first and she never let any ideals get in the way of the practical reality. When I looked around at the misery of the world I could barely believe my luck; I must have done something very good to have this in my life. Our children became the centre of her world and in human terms that is how it should be. Mother love has an unselfish quality rarely seen outside that relationship. It touches and inspires us and in seeing this we get a glimpse of the possibility of unconditional love. Jane was the archetypal mother and I thought of her as the best wife ever. The whole of our children's childhood years were the most special of my life. We were meant to be together and nothing and no one would ever part us – at least that's what I truly believed at the time. We were the perfect couple; people would comment how much they could feel our love. I would never have envisaged that it would be me to break us up.

## THE EMPEROR

I continued to make a good living with the business and increasingly put energy into the spiritual group. There was a feeling of a mission about it; at times I felt it was the most important thing I could do – after all, what could be better than promoting a spiritual way of life? I came across many cranks and many blind alleys. God there are some flakes in the world! I researched other forms of spiritual models, took various courses, spoke to endless people and worked really hard. Fortunately, Jane was sympathetic to my stance, and I had the strength and love of my family.

Exploring the entire subject brought to bear my whole feelings of spirituality on a personal level. So many people with different ideas. Some believed we were star children and were waiting to come home; some took a psychological approach and believed that spirituality was merely part of our nature, some were fundamentalist and adhered to a particular model of belief that probably had not changed for hundreds and thousands of years. And then there were the "new agers", who did not seem to mind what they did or whom they followed, but seemed less good at taking responsibility for their own growth. Mystics down the ages tell us that the truth is within, that we are connected to God, we just have to listen. I tried to listen and sometimes the messages came so clear I could do little else but to follow them. Sometimes I was less sure.

Jane and the family allowed me to feel the Emperor – empowered, the father, the male, the action force and drive that is evident at this stage of growth. At this time, I was able to provide material comfort for the family and establish a good structure for us to live. And in the echo of that kind of determination, I could catch sight of a greater determination to rise beyond the physical world to do something more altruistic. But the real inner strength I needed was not yet in place.

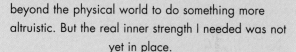

*I dreamt my lady came and found me dead, strange dream that gives a dead man leave to think. And breathed such life with kisses in my lips that I revived and was an Emperor*

Shakespeare, *Romeo and Juliet*

I used my business acumen to make money for the group and that was not always as easy as it sounded. It's one thing to make money in a normal business but in an area that is not supposed to think about money, it was hard. However, money came in for the group and I took very little out of it, barely expenses most years. I spent very much more time on this than my other business, but I believed it to be sound. I had good people working on it and it seemed to be ticking along nicely. I should have realized that if you take your eye off the ball it bounces away.

I explored and researched teachers and gurus, many of whom I discovered were not what they seemed such as those who would stand up and speak pretty words on a platform then get off and be abusive to their colleagues. If spirituality is to work, surely it must work all the time. You can't just be holy on a Sunday and think it's right to get away with bad behaviour every other day in your home with your family and friends. I felt very strongly about this and was so very grateful for the loving wonderful family I had. I would never do something like that I thought.

## THE LOVERS

The years went on, the children grew. I was so proud of them even through their teenage angst. Life was ticking away, I felt I was happy, which makes what occurred even more puzzling.

I was at a conference, one of many I had attended over the years. Adele came in late, but we got talking in the break. She had a remarkably similar view on life to me; she liked the same things and thought the same way. She was married and so was I and at first there did not seem to be any harm in exchanging contact addresses, after all we were in the same field. We e-mailed each other about various aspects of the work. I really enjoyed our exchanges and thoughts, and then she phoned, she was in my area, could we meet up. Again at this stage it all seemed so innocent. We had a drink, talked about the work, and then got on to subjects more personal. She was bored, unhappy with her life, her husband was a workaholic, and she was lonely. This brought out the protective element in me. I felt she was far too beautiful to be treated in such a way. Something about the way the light caught her that evening made my stomach jump; I watched her face, her smile, I enjoyed her intelligence and then suddenly to my horror I realized I was very attracted to her physically. We parted saying we would meet again; I went home thinking that I must stop this now and I had every intention of doing so. I threw my arms around my wife and thanked her for her love; she seemed surprised at my burst of affection. How could I even be thinking about another woman? But the trap was set and I was hooked.

I could not stop thinking about Adele and I did

*But love is blind, and lovers cannot see the pretty follies that themselves commit*

Shakespeare, *The Merchant of Venice*

not put a stop to it. She was younger than my wife. I was at that certain mid-life age and Adele so excited me I could hardly work or think. Maybe it will blow away I thought naively; I let it progress. Months went by; my wife knew something was wrong but I just put it down to pressure of work. I would sneak off to meet Adele whenever I could, usually once or twice a week. We wanted to be together; I could not stand being apart. This made me make comparisons with Jane and for the first time in 20 years I would find fault, pick fights. I did anything that justified me wanting to be with Adele. My marriage had always been so good. Why was this happening? I even persuaded myself it was karma that Adele and I were destined to be together; why else would it happen?

Excuses abounded and Adele wanted me to leave my wife and be with her. What to do? I was in torment; agonizing days, weeks and months went by. I could not connect with spirit; I could not even meditate; I was angry with God. What is the purpose, why is this happening? What could I do? How do you choose between two women you love? The passion was overwhelming. In heightened emotions one day I blurted it out to Jane. She was very quiet, no recriminations just an awful look that said "Why?" The day I left home it felt like my soul was ripped apart but Adele was there waiting – a new life, a good life, a better life.

## THE DEVIL

The children took it badly; my son would not speak to me, my daughter came to visit and pleaded with me to return. "Dad, why are you doing this? You and Mum had something wonderful; everyone said so." I looked at my lovely daughter; I remembered the day she was born. I loved her so much. All I could find to say was "I had to go."

The first few weeks and months with Adele were intense, wonderful. We could not take our hands off each other. We had a constant wonderful sensuous passion. I took time off work and dropped the spiritual group. My thoughts and mind were dissipated; I could not concentrate. It's difficult to describe my feelings. At the time I would have told you I was blissfully happy; when I look back, I realize I was in a kind of madness that I had little power to resist.

We made love endlessly, getting more and more experimental – animal, lusty sex. My God, it took me over; I was obsessed. Nothing else seemed to matter. I lost contact with my friends and had minimal contact with my children. I barely did any work. I was caught in the chains of passion. As the months went on we started to argue. I can't say why. Our fights were just as passionate as our sex and we would throw plates, scream and shout, but it always ended in us having sex so it made it seem all right. Days would go by and we would fight again. At first it never occurred to me that there was anything wrong in the relationship. After all, the passion was still there; we wanted to be together. If I was honest with myself, I would have known how miserable I became. I begun to feel disempowered in everything except lovemaking. All the things that I thought we shared became inconsequential, but I still wanted

her. Months went by, I became a shadow of myself, nothing seemed to flow. I could not be bothered with the business and was often abusive on the phone with colleagues. I got more and more depressed, I did not want to talk to anyone, I was sliding into an abyss and getting deeper.

*Tell the truth and shame the devil*

Shakespeare, *Henry V Part I*

Our fears, our lust and greed overpower us when experiencing this stage. The feelings are so strong it is a rare man that has the necessary power to resist. We think we have something great, we call it love but it is merely a shadow of the real thing. It deceives, grieves and overwhelms us and somewhere deep inside we know it is not right, but we dare not admit it. We make excuses, lie, to others and ourselves. It is fear, which must at some time be faced. It must be driven to the light so it may dissolve and we can finally see the falseness of the devil's promise. How can it be done?

When Adele and I rowed I once caught my reflection in the mirror; it was like looking at someone else, someone dark. Was this really what I had become? I did not dare think too much of the spirituality. The fights got worse and one day she stormed off saying she needed a break. I pleaded with her to return; it would get better I implored, I could not live without her. God I was pathetic, I would have done anything; she had me in her power but I did not care.

# THE HANGED MAN

She got an apartment nearby but we continued our relationship; neither one of us had power to resist but she began to tell me she was more busy and couldn't see me very much. I would wait, like a dog on his mistress's lead. When we were together is was a bit easier; we argued less, but then we spent most of the time making love, which was still wonderfully intoxicating. Because I spent more time alone, I started grieving for my life, my children, my home. I had heard from the children that Jane had started an M.A. and was ploughing her energy into her studies. Sometimes I felt guilty but it was too painful to think about what I had done. Adele waved the carrot of us being together for always; inside both of us probably knew this would just never happen. It was much much later that I was finally able to admit that the love Adele and I had was not a soul connection but just another fatal attraction.

*The ancient saying is no heresy; hanging and wiving goes by destiny*

Shakespeare, *The Merchant of Venice*

Having delegated much of my business to others, I was having minimal contact with work, but being so much on my own, my mind wanted stimulus. I started reading up on different cultural beliefs, I made notes which turned into pages that I knew could be a book. There seemed to me some link between the faiths, something that was mystically present in all of them. I studied many religious documents, found interesting articles that touched on similarities. Perennial philosophy is fairly well documented but many religious texts had been distorted over the years and the dogma of the beliefs were obscured making any direct comparison almost impossible to authenticate. However, when I looked into the experience of spirituality, I begun to see some patterns emerging. Models of the spiritual pathway had similar processes. What I did not appreciate at the time was that I was searching, searching not just for some academic proof of God within everything, but some proof that God was in me. But at this time Adele would always come first. I would drop everything as soon as she rang and when we arranged to meet I would be on tenterhooks all day with expectation. Then no work was done. Sometimes I tried to talk to Adele about my research but she seemed only to pay lip service to my thoughts. To Adele the deeper things meant doing good when she could. There is nothing wrong with that but I had noticed she only did these things when it suited her. Maybe that's unfair but it's how it seemed; in fact she only did anything when it suited her – even making love to me.

There are times in our lives when decisions have to be made, it is hard to let go of anything whether it is an intellectual idea, fantasy, love or some precious attitude on life. If we do not we are doomed to a life of being blown hither and thither by the dictates of the wind. Somewhere inside us all is knowledge of what is really right for us. Somewhere we know what our soul really needs and it is often not what we desire or would wish. We may curse God or the universe; but there's no point – ultimately sooner or later we have to take responsibility for what we know to be true. The distress this may cause can create a darkness that could swallow us up, but the human spirit calls softly at first, it gets louder and gradually, finally, it draws us home.

## THE MOON

How many nights I just sat and watched the moon. I got to know every movement of the stars. Sometimes it gave me great comfort to know that the circle of the stars would revolve and be there. Sometimes I would just curse and think we all were like hamsters trapped on a wheel. What was the meaning of life?

The mysterious depths of our unconscious come to entice us to give a glimmer of a meaning and then it's gone. My thoughts were often chaotic; sometimes I thought they were genius, sometimes I thought I was in madness. I was awash with emotions in a sea of consciousness that I just did not seem to be able to grasp. It felt like I was swimming in an ocean that had no shores, no boundaries. I was powerless to do anything but wait. Sometimes the torment of this was so great I wanted to drown in these waters. Shifting moods and confusion, I could not quite grasp what it was I was supposed to be

thinking, feeling or doing. I was in a wasteland of uncertainty, a place I had never experienced. Sometimes a thought would come into my head that seemed plausible – some dim awareness – and then it would dissipate, dissolve into the waters of illusion.

*O swear not by the moon, th'inconstant moon that monthly changes in her circled orb, Lest that thy love prove likewise variable*

Shakespeare, Romeo and Juliet

## THE HIGH PRIESTESS

Through the murky waters of emotion she would come, the priestess, the energy of the unconscious and I caught a glimpse of daylight. The things that we believe are reality are shown in bold awareness of what they truly are. Our intuition slowly grows. The unconscious holds the secrets of ourselves. The priestess within us knows; she is that part of us that knows the secrets of our inner world. She sometimes comes by night in the form of dreams so that we catch some reality and she comes to us by strange happenings that have profound meanings. Like the moon of emotions we cannot immediately grasp it, but unlike the moon it is not the nebulous energy of dissipated emotions it is a sense of knowing, a conscious realisation of what we have to do. It is a call to truth, which sets off an opening to a more healthy path. Gradually our dreams take shape, our sense of something more than the obvious remains. She is persistent that priestess part of ourselves, she will never give up or leave us, she is constant. We begin to listen, we finally begin to hear. But it comes with confusion out of the murky waters of emotion but with the alarming reality of the truth that we have been unable to face. At this stage there is very little evidence of action in our lives. From the outside it might seem we are doing nothing and in earthly terms this may be true. But what is going on below the surface is more profound that any action or movement we do in the physical world. How we think and know ourselves will change our lives for ever. A small shift in perception will have the effect of altering the whole trajectory of our lives. My perceptions of me were altered 360°. I would never be the same. Somehow I just had to trust my newly born intuition and that it would lift me from the ashes to fly once more.

*No automatic system can be intelligently run by automatons - or by people who dare not assert human intuition, human autonomy, human purpose*

Lewis Mumford

## STRENGTH

I started to get really angry at everything and everybody. There was a rage burning up inside me; even with everyday phone calls I noticed my tolerance level was low. I dare not take it out on Adele – I wanted to keep her too much – so sometimes I would just take off, drive off in the middle of the night. I wanted to hit out, hurt anything. There was a beast within me which I could barely handle and sometimes did not handle at all. My body came out in rashes. I refused to see a doctor, I guess I feared he might suspect my rage and put me away. Nothing seemed rational and although I continued my research, I often ended up tearing up the paper I had written on. This could not go on; sometimes I felt I would explode with the pressure. Like Forrest Gump I took some therapy in walking and walking and walking. Hours of it. I can't even say where I went. I deliberately exhausted myself so when I got home I just collapsed into bed to find some comfort in sleep. This did not always work, my sleep patterns altered and my dreams were nightmare monsters. One dream I had a lot was of huge beasts that would try to devour me. I had read a bit about dreams; I knew that anything in a dream could be an aspect of yourself. If the beasts I dreamed of were an aspect of me I was in big trouble!

I was like a child demanding that the world revolved around me. Patience was nil. Even standing at a check-out queue made me angry. I was aware that in energy terms my beast was incredibly strong and it occurred to me that if that energy could somehow be managed and used productively it could really do great things. How I could do it in this state was another matter. I was pushing Adele to do things she did not want. I wanted her to go away with me for several months. She told me she could not leave her job. I was sure if she wanted to she could.

*As thy days, so shall thy strength be*

Deuteronomy 33:25

The key to transformation is that individuals own their lives and what they do and that they look, really look at reality, whatever that might produce. As the months went on I felt more and more like the sacrificial lamb. I began slowly but surely to realize that the relationship with Adele was not going to work. I tried to fool myself for a while but once awareness comes it does not leave. Somehow I must find the strength to sacrifice my passion for a better life. To seek a better truth. Making the decision was very hard. Unlike the direct action man of the past I felt emaciated, inadequate. I had left my wife and my friends; I had abandoned my work and my spiritual contacts. I had torn many lives apart for what? Just to say it did not work. When people say let go of your ego they have no idea what they are asking; letting go of your ego and pride feels as though your whole self is being seared with flames. I had always thought I'd win. I never thought I would lose. I always thought I was right. At last with all the courage I could find I did what I should have done before: I told Adele it was over and in doing so I walked away from the dream of a life with a perfect woman. Perfection, like fantasy, does not exist.

# THE TOWER

I realized I wanted to go home, home to Jane. I had increasingly been going over the past. When we were together it was the happiest time of my life. I remembered her love, her compassion, the wife, the mother, the friend. I knew that love was real. I'd made a mistake but our love would survive. I tried to phone Jane over several days but I just got her answer machine. I phoned our daughter. "Mum's away; she's gone to America for six months to work and she's found a man. It's great to see her happy again," she said. As I put the phone down the awful realization that I had lost the best person in my life seeped into my consciousness. I was still in shock when, minutes later, the phone rang again and I automatically pressed the button. It was my business manager. "Where the hell have you been?" he said. "I have been trying to reach you for days. This is serious, we need to talk." I told him I was going away. "I don't think you will when I tell you what has happened."

I met him an hour later; he had a determined and pale face. I knew immediately it was bad. He explained that in delegating, my business had been destroyed. I laughed. "Its worth millions," I said. "It was," came the reply. Some kind of embezzlement had occurred. "What's the damage?" I asked. "I'm afraid I have to tell you you have lost everything." At first the words did not sink in. "Come on, there must be something left," I said in desperation. "No, nothing; in fact, it's so serious we could be personally liable. All your accounts are under investigation." "Why? How?" I said. "I'm sorry to say this to a man when he's down, but if you had spent more time looking after the business rather than chasing rainbows this would not have happened. You used to be so on the ball, Chris, where did it go?"

*Nor stony tower, nor walls of beaten brass, nor airless dungeon, nor strong links of iron can be retentive to the strength of spirit*

Shakespeare, *Julius Caesar*

Hindsight is a wonderful thing; looking back on how it occurred it would be obvious to a simpleton that disaster would be likely to strike. I used to be good at business, so much the man of action; where was that person now? And more importantly what the hell was I going to do?

On that day my whole life collapsed. I had nothing – no job, no home, no love. My world collapsed utterly. I walked for a while then I sat down on a grass verge with my head in my hands; I watched the sun set and that evening, exhausted, alone and afraid, as though some invisible lightening flash had struck me, I was laid bare. Suddenly I saw myself, really saw myself for the very first time. This brilliant piercing light filled my whole being. It was like a huge electric shock. The light was too bright; I had nowhere to hide, I had to see myself. I was shaken to the core. No peripheral masks, denials, or prevarication would come to my aid. All the constructs of my life were shattered. All previous ideals, impressions of what I wanted to be and not what I really was were dissolved. They say one can get instant realization; what they don't say is what leads up to that point. At that moment I surrendered, finally surrendered to life. A light filled me, it surrounded me and in my vulnerability I finally found peace.

## HIEROPHANT: HIGH PRIEST

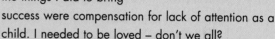

I did not want to deceive myself about anything again. I was scrupulous about it; I even underwent psychotherapy to see if there was anything I had missed. The therapist and I spent time talking about the family, patterns of behaviour that started as a child. We talked about conflict and how I dealt with it. I acknowledged the male quirk that only wants to please women. Have you any idea how this one trait in a man disables him? I learned about men, I learned about women. I learned about relationships and I learned about me. I learned that the things I did to bring success were compensation for lack of attention as a child. I needed to be loved – don't we all?

I did not want to leave any stone unturned. I gained enormous self discipline and began to take mastery of my desires. There is a deep part of ourselves that is our own teacher, our own guru, but how many of us really listen to the inner part of ourselves that really has the truth? Yet it is there all the time in the background. We know, we really do know, so why don't we listen? Are we really so afraid of the truth? This might mean changing your way of life but isn't it better to live with truth and not lies? Maybe we do not have the strength to administer what we know to be right. My invocation was "Divine light of consciousness, open me up to greater possibilities, to greater truths, and give me the wisdom to deal with it."

*Wisdom is the principal thing,*
*therefore get wisdom*
Proverbs 4:7

# THE HERMIT

The lawyers were dealing with the business; it was not going to be quick. I had no bank account, but I did have a very expensive car. I drove to the sales room and sold it for cash. I went to the airport and bought a ticket to Spain. There was a place in the mountains I'd always loved; it was as good a place as any to be. I rented a small villa that looked over a valley with no other houses in sight. I looked out and saw the beauty of the landscape. I was still bereaved and in shock. My days were spent doing simple things – shopping, cooking, walking, a bit of gardening and hours of just sitting. Even in my angst I was able to realize it is still a beautiful world.

I felt like a hermit in his cave. Quiet contemplation. I felt strangely at peace. I had connected with what could only be called some force or deep energy source that was not outside myself but was within. I realized that in some shape or form I had felt this all my life. But why did I not really listen to it before? It hummed inside me like an ever-present engine. Was it my soul? Bit by bit I felt myself align and attune to it. When it really was active I felt invincible, unafraid of anything that life might bring. It would sometimes slip but knowing where to find it, gradually it became easier and easier to connect with it again. It was comfortable, safe, safer than anything on an external level. I had a metaphorical lantern to guide me but the light was not external to myself, it was within. It had always been there but like most people I sometimes had not known, sometimes I ignored it but mostly I let the noise of a busy world distract me from it. Contact with this deep inner being made me aware that on a soul level I, the real I, could never be destroyed and I knew therefore I was indestructible.

*The mind can weave itself warmly into the cocoon of its own thoughts and dwell a hermit anywhere*

James Russell Lowell

# DEATH

In those months away in Spain it was like being a different person. I had always been very active, always looking for the next deal, but the time spent with Adele, and my state of mind at that time, dissolved the man I was – or at least that's how it felt. When our life is destroyed what do we do? Some people would try to pick up the pieces and try again. Deep inside me I knew I could never live the same life. My priorities had changed. I had no desire to make money for the sake of it. I'd had the life style that money brings and it held no attraction for me. I was empty. I lived the life of a monk: walking in the hills, speaking to few people. Frequently I sat in a kind of meditation; I was aware that some invisible process was occurring but I did not know what it was or what it would bring. What I did know was that nothing, absolutely nothing would ever be the same again.

*Of all the wonders that I yet have heard, it seems to me most strange that men should fear, seeing that death a necessary end will come when it will come*

Shakespeare, *Julius Caesar*

With the wonders of technology I was able to trawl the internet and started researching for the book I was continuing to write. Sometimes I was excited by a particular finding or thought. Sometimes I thought I was on to something really important, other times I just thought it was mediocre at best. I was in mourning. Not just bereavement of relationships and my business but bereavement of a part of my self that was gone for ever. The child part, the bit that wants its own way. The bit that is "I must have, it's mine". I felt naked, deprived of the mere falsehood of my previous existence. The masks I had worn were torn away. The persona I had previously used was gone. I had no coat of protection; I stood bare. In those months I thought a lot about my actions, thoughts and feelings. When we look, really look at ourselves without the pretence of having to think we are right or we are Mister Nice Guy, all sorts of things emerge from the depths. I could see how selfish I had been in my life. The person that was supposed to do all the right things for people was really only doing it so I felt good about me. The egoist sense that I was something special or different from the rest was an illusion. I examined my motives. When illusion and delusions are shattered and we see things for the first time and realize our motives were not as we thought, it is devastating and I could easily have plunged into self indulgence of what an awful person I must be, but we can only work from what we know and I had not known. I berated myself a great deal. What a bastard I was to my family, my wife, my friends; but as time wore on I realized the person I had hurt most was me. I could not drown myself in regrets, what I could do was make it better. In death there is birth and renewal and in any birth or beginning there is death of something else. Some rite of passage was occurring, I wasn't sure what, but out of the depths of despair a tiny glimmer of hope survived.

## THE WHEEL

And so the ever turning of the wheel of life moves on and on. I felt a bit like you feel when you leave home for the first time. The loss of a home and all that it means; the loss of a woman in my life felt like losing one's mother, but I'm no psychologist. I was like a newborn baby and was aware that only through time could I begin to form my feelings, my true feelings. When I looked backwards I did not like myself; I did not much like many of the things I had done in my life. I berated the fact that I had been so unaware. But that was the old me; I had to somehow put that behind me, forgive the past, forgive myself, let go and walk on. I felt empty and yet there was this inner light, revealing to me that my life was a blank page and on it I could write whatever I wanted.

It was a full year before I came back to England. The dealings on the business were still being sorted out. It seemed there was at least something to salvage, albeit very little. The problem for me was I had no desire to start another business. The whiz kid was gone. I had no stomach for the driving force needed to push that kind of animal forward. What would I do with my life? I had to work: what could I do, what did I want to do? The new me was still forming and I did not know what that would manifest in the material world. I would have to trust in the process. I had to be OK about not knowing, not always trying to solve things, just be.

It was good to see my children again. They seemed to have their lives together much more than me, so something productive had come from my existence on this earth. A friend let me stay in his flat and I finished the book. A good thing about being a successful businessman was that I had many contacts in all sorts of areas. I knew a publishing firm and I presented my work. I wasn't happy but the despair was finally subsiding. Most of all I felt that whatever happened to me it really did not matter. Everything we experience happens for us to learn. Everything we do teaches us something.

I was trundling on when I received a call from the publisher. "There's a lot of work and some rewrites to do with this but I think its worth a shot," he said. I was amazed. It had been written for my own discovery to find out more about what really is behind the spiritual concepts old and new. The book came out in the autumn and sales were good. My publisher called. He wanted a chat. He'd had a call from a TV station; they thought the book was well researched and wanted to run a short series. Apparently the publisher had told them of my abilities and they wanted me to be involved.

Life has many twists and turns. Opportunities come and it's up to us to grasp them. I had nothing to lose and although these were very new waters for me, I was willing to give it a try.

*Let us sit and mock the good housewife fortune from her wheel, that her gifts may henceforth be bestowed equally*

Shakespeare, *As You Like It*

## JUSTICE

I had discovered myself; now I was being asked to create an image for publicity. I could not pretend; if they did not like me as I was I really could not do it. I had in the last few months found an inner peace that I had never felt before. I did not want to lose it for flimflam. But we are in a material world; I had to do some work and I believed in the book I had written. Life, it seemed, was presenting me with an opportunity to express my thoughts to a wider audience, and on one level it seemed too good to be true. Life is ironic; if this had been ten years ago or even five, I would have been jumping for joy. Now I just felt wary of all the limelight. There were promotions, interviews all over the place; it seemed I had struck a chord and the subject of contemporary spirituality was unfolding with interest coming from many diverse areas ranging from the new age to academia. Of course, not surprisingly, I trod on some people's toes. I got lots of good letters but some that said how dare you suggest you can be spiritual if you don't believe in our deity. I personally had no belief and basically took the stance that anyone's cultural background was probably the best method towards his or her spiritual roots. But it's only half the picture. The real essence is manifested within the experience of the individual. This does not sit too well with set dogmas that upon investigation often come more from the people subsequent to the original roots of the religion.

How to keep balance in my own feelings as I was getting more and more attention and admiration? I was told I was a natural behind the camera. Initially I took it all with a pinch of salt; I thought they were just flattering me. But as more and more people said the same thing, I started believing my own press. Men and women of standing told me they thought this was a really important work. It's easy to be at one with yourself if you are on your own; with all the excitement of the success it was more difficult. However, intelligent understanding of what was occurring just about kept my feet on the ground; we all have to learn to think clearly and to cultivate and maintain a balanced mind. We have to learn to cope with whatever life throws at us. We have to keep a sense of self that is the core truth in amongst the hustle of the world that can cloak our true being. In many ways it's like being a tightrope walker. We cannot afford to loose concentration on the moment in which we exist, or we may find living in the present enables us to be aware and in balance it enables us to walk on.

In amongst all this I was also dealing with court proceedings from my old business. The culprits were finally coming to trial. I did not feel angry towards them; in many ways I now believed they did me a favour. If I still had the business I would be stuck in a world in which I no longer belonged. As I walked finally from the court seeing the motif of Athena's scales, it felt as though life was telling me the most important thing is a balanced mind, heart and body.

*It is enthroned in the hearts of kings, it is an attribute to God himself, And earthly power doth then show likest God's when mercy seasons justice*

Shakespeare, *The Merchant of Venice*

## TEMPERANCE

Time is the great healer they say and I had found some kind of peace, but my emotions were still frayed. I actually started to believe I would never have another relationship. How could I take the risk? Without the burden of the emotions I felt safe, free. All those feeling getting in the way of life. I really did not think I could go through it all again. Life however allows us to forget the feeling of the pain even if it does not allow us to forget we have had it. We can remember it happened, how and when, but the feeling does not stay with us. It's probably similar to how a woman can experience the pain of childbirth, and forget it enough to do it again.

*Time hath, my lord a wallet at his back wherein he puts alms for oblivion*

Shakespeare, *Troilus and Cressida*

Gradually as time wore on the pain subsided. I was comfortable in my life. I had a good relationship with my children, the work from the book had all kinds of spinoffs that enabled me to travel all over the world. I was comfortable in my own skin, happy to give advice when asked but equally happy to stay quiet. I felt the need to have quiet times often. I would either take myself off to some remote area or sometimes I would go on retreat to various monasteries or places of rest. I gave myself quality time. I learned not to drink too much; I ate well with food that suited me. I exercised and swam a lot. My life was balanced and yet, in retrospect, only because I did not have the encumbrance of an emotional life. I was into my middle age and time seems different when you are older; you start thinking about old age and death. Time becomes more precious; you think how to fill the last part of your life.

My daughter announced she was to be married. I liked the guy; he was sound, easy to talk to, if a little naive, but who isn't at that age? He made her happy: that was the main thing. The wedding was on a bright summer's day. As I led my daughter up the aisle I caught sight of a woman in Madonna blue; something about her movement attracted me; she turned – it was Jane. I had, of course, spoken with Jane about the arrangements, but I hadn't seen her for a couple of years. The years had treated her well; she looked bright, empowered. I remembered why I had been attracted to her and my heart missed a beat. At the reception we talked. She was doing well, her life had taken different turns. She had a job that gave her satisfaction. It did not quite seem the appropriate time to ask but I found myself asking if she was happy in her personal life. There is no one special she said. "But I thought you had a man in your life?" I said. "I did, but it didn't last; he was a good man but ..." she paused, "You are a hard act to follow." "I'm not the same man as I was; things and people change," I said. "But the essence stays the same," she said, and drifted away to talk to relatives.

It was a happy day, filled with laughter and good food. I had forgotten the wonderful feeling of being with the family, that comfort, warmth and friendship. I did not want it to go away. After the bride and groom had gone I sought Jane out. "Would you consider having lunch with me tomorrow?" Her head turned to one side and she smiled. "OK."

## THE CHARIOT

We found a good country pub and sat in the sunshine. We chatted about the kids, what they were doing and how they had grown up intelligent and healthy. I looked at her and said "I still love you, you know." "Why did you leave then?" she said. "Oh, Jane, how can I answer that? I just had to. It's been hard, you know." "Why?" she said. "Because it didn't work with you and Adele?" There was a trace of bitterness in her voice which I ignored. "Partly," I replied, "But it's difficult to talk about; I've been through some kind of transformation." "Yes," she said. "I see the grey hairs on your head!" We laughed. "No, I've achieved some profound awareness that means I will never be the same again." I opened up; I had forgotten how easy it was to talk to her. "I'm not the same either, Chris," she said. "Being on my own taught me many things about myself, it made me examine life, too".

Men and women are so different; how do we ever get together? The action of the man, the receptivity of a woman. The emotional needs of a woman and the emotional needs of a man are different. A man needs to have a sense of worth, a standing. A woman needs to know she is loved. But somehow at this time of my life I began to see the feminine side of myself. I had abandoned the warrior male for something more spiritual. Ironically, Jane seemed to have done the reverse, she seemed powerful and direct and she had drive and determination of which I had previously been unaware. I only knew I wanted to be with her.

We met again and surprisingly our friendship picked up as though it had never left. She let me talk about the spiritual shifts, the torment of the relationship with Adele, the business and all that I felt. I wanted to be with her, but would the past get in the way? If I rationalized it, I would say there must have been something missing in our relationship to fall for Adele; or was it just the male lust? This is hard for any man to acknowledge and very few do. Did I really go off with Adele just for passion? It's a question I felt uneasy about confronting; I daren't look. The only answer I could come up with was I don't know. There had been no real crisis in my relationship with Jane and yet I had been bored, restless. Could it have been that life presented me with the situation that enabled me, albeit with some pain, to bring about the changes of consciousness. Can life be so cruel? And yet do any of us really put ourselves deliberately through such turmoil unless we are pushed? I doubt it. We want things the same, familiar, but change is part of life, change is necessary, change instigates movement and life is movement. Had I invoked the emotional conflict myself? Had some deeper part of me known I needed change? But out from it all I had fought a battle both in the inner and outer worlds and come to some equilibrium. Could I dare to put myself in such a space again? And then there were the human considerations; what if it didn't work with Jane, that is supposing she wanted me back? Could we both go through the terrors of another break up? My feeling persisted, I wanted to be with her.

> *But at my back I always hear time's winged chariot hurrying near. And yonder all before us lie deserts of vast eternity*
>
> Andrew Marvell

## THE STAR

Jane seemed so independent these days; she had really got her life together. She was away for several weeks on a working trip. What if she found someone else? What if she just wanted us to be good friends? I rationalized what was the worst thing that could happen? She could say no. Would that really be so bad, I asked myself. After all, we both had separate lives, we both had gone through a massive amount of self discovery over the last few years. She had told me that after I left she went through a dark period that made her realize she needed to examine her life and herself also. She had reassessed her whole life and she had realized that she had never really looked at herself outside her role as daughter, wife and mother. This process brought confusion and she simply did not know what she wanted from life because she did not know who she was. I understood this feeling well. It seems that most people are constantly playing a role, that may or may not have anything to do with who they really are. They are born in a certain family, in a certain environment where people have certain norms of behaviour. We all automatically take on these norms just as if it is right. Most people never even consider the possibility that there may be something else. And when that hammer hits home that all is not what it seems, it is extremely uncomfortable. Most people are too frightened to look. Too much embedded in the status quo. They do not want to change, they do not want their models of life to be disturbed, and who can blame them? But it means they are forever moving through time living a construct that they have never questioned. It may or may not be a good

*When the sun shall lose its light, when the stars shall fall down from the firmament, when the mountains shall remove from their places ... then shall a soul comprehend what it has shaped*

The Koran

construct but it certainly isn't one that they have thought out or created themselves. To be self determining we need to look within and be brave enough to open Pandora's box. We may find things inside we do not like and have to adjust accordingly. However, alongside the darker aspects of self, hope is also present in Pandora's box and hope is a quality within us that despite disease, imprisonment or terrible disappointments allows us to carry this spark of light that intuitively tells us that eventually we will be OK. Yes, it's scary to look inside ourselves without a clue as to what is inside, but what is more scary is that people are walking around playing roles they did not create and even worse do not realize they are doing it.

I had hope but hope is fragile, with all the possibilities of fear and disasters. But to have no hope is to live with gloom, to allow ourselves the self indulgence of feeling sorry for ourselves and feel that nothing will or could work. Is hope connected to our soul I wondered, and what of those awful stories of people whose child goes missing and they wait and wait, sometimes for years only to be told their child is dead? I put that thought aside as I endeavoured to keep my eyes fixed on the vague, irrational and inexplicable sense that soon there would be a dawning of a new and wonderful time. In my heart I now knew that Jane and I were partners – for better, for worse. I only hoped she knew that as well.

## THE SUN

I had been commissioned to write another book and I was also being asked to appear on TV as an expert in the field. Success was good, but I had known the other side, and consequently knew that both success and failure are impostors; they mean nothing. Everything is transient, everything changes, particularly in our fast-moving celebrity culture where if we have some fame it is merely a speck of dust in the clutter we call life. We might think we can change the world and we can, each and everyone of us. But we change our world by the energy we give out each day and good energy can be emitted just as easily in the supermarket, and in any day-to-day activity. The world is changed not so much by luminaries who win prizes or look good, but by all those good things that are done each day, by all of us. What is success? Maybe true success is really love, not the love of desire but that of unconditionality. At its best it seems to release a clasp that allows us to be free; it dispels the dark. Something in the human psyche pushes out from the weeds a tiny blossom that emerges into light. It might remain unnoticed or little understood but it has driven humanity through the millennia. It is the indomitable spirit of the human soul, which we can never analyze or know, but love is the closest we get; perhaps that is why all cultures speak of it. The human heart, the sacred heart releases us from bondage and allows us to journey home.

Jane was due back from the States on the Friday. Apart from a couple of e-mails we had not had any contact for several weeks. I phoned her on the Saturday; she seemed surprised to hear my voice.

*We make guilty of our disasters, the sun, the moon and stars, as if we were villains on necessity, fools by heavenly compulsion*

Shakespeare, *King Lear*

We talked about her trip and the success of my ventures. "Can we have dinner?" I said. There was a pause. "OK." Love, they say, is not everything, and in a material world that is quite possibly true, but without love there is very little meaning, very little purpose and little joy. Love has many meanings; we can love our pets, our favourite TV programme, we can love our friends, our lovers; but depth love is not so common and it fills our whole being with light. Not the light of passion or emotional support, not the highs and the lows but the constant eternal flame that is ever alive. Dear God, I was so thankful that my love was still alive, even with the possibility that I would be rejected. Was it St. Augustine that said, "There is a place in people's hearts that does not exist into which pain enters so that it might exist."? The pain of love can be torment, but somehow as it subsides it allows more knowledge, more strength and eventually more love. I knew I would love, really love, Jane all my life and somewhere within all my doubts I knew she would always love me too.

It was autumn; the colours were particularly beautiful as I drove with her to a country restaurant. It was tasteful; good food and quiet tables. I didn't know how to start the conversation. "I love you, Jane; I think I have always loved you even through the last few years." She started to speak but I said, "I want to be with you the rest of our lives. Can you forgive the past and be my wife?"

# JUDGEMENT

She looked shocked. She did not speak. At last she held my hand. "I love you too but you must give me time to digest this. I'm sorry I can't say anything at the moment; let's just enjoy the meal." I have no idea what food I ate that night or how I got home; the rest of the evening was a blur. When I dropped her off she said she would be in contact.

During those next few days I examined the past we had shared; I examined my motives once again. I had now done extensive therapy on myself, but each step of the way creates a different view. If we change, even slightly, our whole perception is altered, and consequently the trajectory of our lives alters also. Was it madness to try to get back with Jane? We had in the last few years done our own thing. We had both changed. Maybe we had changed too much for it to work. Could the very real love we once had and still had, be the lighthouse that would help us through the next stage?

Jane phoned three days later. "We need to talk," she said. We met at her place and she started to tell me about all her feelings when I left. She had never really talked about this before. She told me of her resentment, her grief, her feeling that somehow she must have been at fault. For months she spiralled downward finding it extremely difficult to be positive. It was at that point she had taken herself off for counselling. She talked and talked about her feelings and how gradually she came through knowing she was not to blame, and knowing she had a kind of strength that would allow her to move through the torment. She had cut the ties to me she thought permanently. She smiled and said, "Now I know what it must feel like for those women who believe their soldier husbands are dead and they arrive at the door. Sometimes they have remarried or are living a life that they do not want to give up." "Is that what it is like for you, Jane? Do you have a life that you don't want to give up? You know I would put no restrictions on your life." She replied, "Just you being there would alter what I did. I never stopped loving you, but the pain of the separation made me shut the door." My heart stopped when she said this; I was waiting for her to say "No" to my proposal, steeling myself for the worst.

"I never really shut you out completely; I think that is why I couldn't be with another man. But have we learned?" she said. "Have we really learned enough to make this work? Would you go off again?" "Oh Jane," I said. "I would be lying if I gave you definite answers to these questions; the affair with Adele completely took me by surprise. I did not plan or want it. All I can say is that I am older, hopefully wiser, and I will do anything I can to make this work. I love you beyond measure." "Yes," said Jane, "but I couldn't bear it if it happened again." "I know there are no guarantees in life but we can minimize any potential difficulties. We can work together, step by step. We will be honest with each other, we can have a good life." She said nothing for a while, she looked me straight in the eye. "I'm up for an adventure."

*Great men are not always wise neither do the aged understand judgement*

Job 32:9

## THE WORLD

In fairy stories it is always "happily ever after"; would that real life was so certain and always provided us with the perfect future. It was wonderful to explore each other in our new skins; we fitted back into place like a lost jigsaw piece, and we were comfortable together. The children were on their feet and we now had a blank page ahead of us. We could do anything, be anywhere. We had always promised ourselves to travel to places far from tourists, and over several months our plans took shape. Jane took a sabbatical and we began to tour.

*All the world's a stage, and all the men and women merely players*

Shakespeare, *As You Like It*

We started in Canada, then through the States, and down into Mexico and Peru, Colombia and Chile. From there we went to Antarctica where the surreal views of the ice were sublime. We crossed into Africa, and it was while in some fairly treacherous terrain that Jane started feeling unwell. At first we thought it was the effort of all the travel, but she did not improve. I looked at her one day and something told me I had to get her home. We got on the next available flight. Jane was insistent that after some care and a bit of rest she would be back; unfortunately this was not the case. The hospital immediately admitted her; she was seriously ill. I nursed her through her treatment, but to no avail. The end was quick and she died in peace in my arms.

How can a human being dig deep within to rise when beaten down again and again? I could have gone into deep depression, berating the fact that I had lost her, taking on guilt for the pain I had caused; but those absent years allowed us both to grow and we were at peace with ourselves. The individual's challenge is to know and be able to act upon spiritual authenticity. The development of the spiritual self brings a form of unconditionality not just present when we love another human being and he or she loves us, not just when things go well, but also present when tragedy strikes, when our love is unrequited and even with death. This is the alchemy of the human spirit. Somehow, some deep strength emerged and finally gave me acceptance of all life's conditions. I missed her dreadfully and was only grateful that we at least had many months of fun and adventure and we had been so in love.

After the funeral I decided to continue the trip alone; I knew that was what she wanted. I knew I would see her face in every place I went, and in every step I took, and in my heart I would share with her what I found. Through Jane I had learned the real meaning of love. For love to be real it has to survive the hurdles and hardships, it has to forgive, understand and be grateful even when the person is no longer with you. Like an eternal flame, it cannot be destroyed.

We never really know what experiences are there for us to learn and grow. Life is an adventure and adventures have their joys and traumas. And so on a crisp early spring morning when I set out again, I had love in my heart and hope, not knowing what the future would hold, but knowing that whatever happened, with the connectedness of a firm inner strength, I would be able to encounter whatever life would throw at me.

# Index

# Acknowledgments

In writing this book I have tried to put a seemingly nebulous subject into a format that can be easily understood. I hope I have opened the doors for the reader's further research. I have given some background authorities and scientific ideas; most importantly I have quoted real-life experiences to illustrate some of the many processes that one can encounter in spiritual self-development. In the last chapter I use archetypes to bring alive a story of development. This story is fiction, however the characters' experiences are ones that I have encountered in my work time and time again. I hope you find it readable and it helps you understand that your spiritual processes are unique to you and yet you are not alone on your journey.

Many grateful thanks to all below who have helped this work:

Tony Chiva for his King Arthur meditation, and friendship. Angelika Khan for proof reading and support. Terry Larter for his King Arthur meditation. Henry Lincoln for providing me with wonderful quotes in Chapter 7. Freda Northam, my 95 year old next door neighbour for her fantastic mind and wisdom. Alex Soskin for helping me brain storm. Damien Soskin for his encouragement and Rupert Soskin for writing Chapter 2.

Insight and Intuition courses and personal consultations available. Also individual personal training for overseas students.
Contact: Website: www.insightandintuition.com
Email:insight.intuition@blueyonder.co.uk.

**Picture Credits**
Tarot cards on pages 104–105 and 136–57 courtesy of Lo Scarabeo www.loscarabeo.com

Illustration on page 79 by Tim Ashton/Début Art

**References**
Assagioli, R. *Psychosynthesis*, Penguin Books, London 1980.

Avila, T. *Interior Castle*, Image Books, London 1989.

Bloom, W. *The New Age*, Rider Books, London 1991.

Brennan, B.A. *Hands of Light: a Guide to Healing Through the Human Energy Fields*, Bantam Books, USA 1988.

Elkins, D. *Beyond Religion: A Personal Program for Building a Spiritual Life Outside the Walls of Traditional Religion*, Quest Books, USA 1998.

Hardy, A. *The Spiritual Nature of Man*, Clarendon Press, Oxford 1979.

Heelas, P. *The New Age Movement*, Blackwell Publishers, Oxford 1996.

Heron, J. *The Facilitators Handbook*, Kogan Page, London 1989.

Judith, A. *Wheels of Life: A User's Guide to the Chakra System*, Llewellyn Publications, USA 1990.

Jung. C. G. *Collected Works*, Routlege Kegan Paul, London 1960.

Leadbeater, C. W. *The Chakras*, Theosophical Publishing, USA 1996.

Lyons, J.W. "The Mechanism of Dowsing: A Conceptual Model", York University 2003.

Maslow, A. *Towards a Psychology of Being*, John Wiley, Chichester 1999.

Miller, H. *The Definitive Wee Book on Dowsing*, Penwith Press, Cornwall 2002.

Rogers, C. *Freedom to Learn*, Macmillan College Publishing Press, USA 1994.

Rowan, J. *The Transpersonal*, Routledge, London 1993.

Sogyal Rinpoche *The Tibetan Book of Living and Dying*, Random House, London 1992.

Soskin, J. "Insight and Intuition", College of Psychic Studies, London 1996.

Soskin, J. "Psycho-spiritual Studies as Part of a Learning Programme", *Transpersonal Psychology Review*, Vol. 2 No 1, 2003.

Tart, C. *Open Mind, Discriminating Mind; Reflections on Human Possibilities*, Harper Row, London 1989.

Tosey, P. "Energies: A Perspective on Organizations and Change", School of Educational Studies, University of Surrey 1996.

Trevelyan G. *Exploration into God*, Gateway Books, Bath 1991.

Wilber, K. *Integral Psychology: Consciousness, Spirit, Psychology, Therapy*, Shambhala, London 2000.